# COLLINS
# POCKET
# FRENCH
# GRAMMAR

HarperCollins*Publishers*

First published in this edition 1993

© HarperCollins Publishers 1993
**Latest reprint 1995**
ISBN 0 00 470976-4 Paperback

---

*editors*
Lesley A Robertson MA
Lorna Sinclair-Knight BA, PhD

*editorial management*
Vivian Marr

*editorial staff*
Megan Maxwell, Christine Penman

---

*A catalogue record for this book
is available from the British Library*

*Typeset by Tradespools Ltd., Frome, Somerset*

*Printed in Great Britain by
Clays Ltd., St Ives plc*

# INTRODUCTION

Your **Collins Pocket French Grammar** has been designed to give you maximum help in getting to grips with the basic features of the French language. If your knowledge of French grammar is elementary, non-existent or just rusty, this book provides all the essential information you need in a clear, easy-to-understand layout. For those who are already familiar with the structure of French, it provides an invaluable tool for reference and revision.

The book is divided into sections according to part of speech (noun, adjective, adverb etc) or grammar point (sentence structure, translation problems, use of numbers etc) Wherever we have used what may be unfamiliar technical terms, we have tried to give a brief explanation (or illustration) at the relevant point in the text.

One of the most innovative features of this book is the use of colour to highlight the learning points in each section. You can see at a glance exactly which grammar point is being illustrated to make learning easy – and fast!

Another important feature is the clear demarcation of grammatical points, illustrated by numerous examples. For instance, if you turn to page 60, you will see a series of bracketed numbers, (→1) to (→11), in colour throughout the page. These numbers cross-refer you to an example, or group of examples, correspondingly numbered in colour, on page 61. This double-page layout give you maximum accessibility to the grammar point you are trying to learn or revise. And the practical, up-to-date examples help to fix that grammar point firmly in your mind.

The examples which illustrate each grammar point put special emphasis on contemporary French, without ignoring the more literary aspects of the language. Attention has also been paid to areas in which French usage differs from English usage, particularly in the section on sentence structure. And in the section on translation problems, we have tried to show you how to deal with (and avoid) the most common pitfalls.

The fully comprehensive index at the end of the book lists subject references as well as key words in both French and English.

## ABBREVIATIONS USED

| | | | | | |
|---|---|---|---|---|---|
| **ctd.** | continued | **p(p).** | page(s) | **qn** | quelqu'un |
| **fem.** | feminine | **perf.** | perfect | **sb** | somebody |
| **infin.** | infinitive | **plur.** | plural | **sing.** | singular |
| **masc.** | masculine | **qch** | quelque chose | **sth** | something |

# CONTENTS

## Simple Tenses: formation

In French the simple tenses are:

| | |
|---|---|
| Present | (→ **1**) |
| Imperfect | (→ **2**) |
| Future | (→ **3**) |
| Conditional | (→ **4**) |
| Past Historic | (→ **5**) |
| Present Subjunctive | (→ **6**) |
| Imperfect Subjunctive | (→ **7**) |

They are formed by adding endings to a verb stem. The endings show the number and person of the subject of the verb (→ **8**)

The stem and endings of regular verbs are totally predictable. The following sections show all the patterns for regular verbs. For irregular verbs see pp. 74 ff.

## Regular Verbs

There are three regular verb patterns (called conjugations), each identifiable by the ending of the infinitive:

● First conjugation verbs end in **-er** e.g. **donner** to give

● Second conjugation verbs end in **-ir** e.g. **finir** to finish

● Third conjugation verbs end in **-re** e.g. **vendre** to sell

These three conjugations are treated in order on the following pages.

*Continued*

1  **je donne**
I give, I am giving, I do give

2  **je donnais**
I gave, I was giving, I used to give

3  **je donnerai**
I shall give, I shall be giving

4  **je donnerais**
I should/would give, I should/would be giving

5  **je donnai**
I gave

6  **(que) je donne**
(that) I give/gave

7  **(que) je donnasse**
(that) I gave

8  **je donne**            I give
   **nous donnons**        we give
   **je donnerais**        I would give
   **nous donnerions**     we would give

## Simple Tenses: First Conjugation

● The stem is formed as follows:

| TENSE | FORMATION | EXAMPLE |
|---|---|---|
| Present | | |
| Imperfect | | |
| Past Historic | infinitive minus **-er** | **donn-** |
| Present Subjunctive | | |
| Imperfect Subjunctive | | |
| Future | infinitive | **donner-** |
| Conditional | | |

● To the appropriate stem add the following endings:

| | | PRESENT (→**1**) | IMPERFECT (→**2**) | PAST HISTORIC (→**3**) |
|---|---|---|---|---|
| sing. | 1st person | -e | -ais | -ai |
| | 2nd person | -es | -ais | -as |
| | 3rd person | -e | -ait | -a |
| plur. | 1st person | -ons | -ions | -âmes |
| | 2nd person | -ez | -iez | -âtes |
| | 3rd person | -ent | -aient | -èrent |

| | | PRESENT SUBJUNCTIVE (→**4**) | IMPERFECT SUBJUNCTIVE (→**5**) |
|---|---|---|---|
| sing. | 1st person | -e | -asse |
| | 2nd person | -es | -asses |
| | 3rd person | -e | -ât |
| plur. | 1st person | -ions | -assions |
| | 2nd person | -iez | -assiez |
| | 3rd person | -ent | -assent |

| | | FUTURE (→**6**) | CONDITIONAL (→**7**) |
|---|---|---|---|
| sing. | 1st person | -ai | -ais |
| | 2nd person | -as | -ais |
| | 3rd person | -a | -ait |
| plur. | 1st person | -ons | -ions |
| | 2nd person | -ez | -iez |
| | 3rd person | -ont | -aient |

| **1** | PRESENT | | **2** | IMPERFECT | | **3** | PAST HISTORIC |
|---|---|---|---|---|---|---|---|
| je | donne | | je | donnais | | je | donnai |
| tu | donnes | | tu | donnais | | tu | donnas |
| il | donne | | il | donnait | | il | donna |
| elle | donne | | elle | donnait | | elle | donna |
| nous | donnons | | nous | donnions | | nous | donnâmes |
| vous | donnez | | vous | donniez | | vous | donnâtes |
| ils | donnent | | ils | donnaient | | ils | donnèrent |
| elles | donnent | | elles | donnaient | | elles | donnèrent |

| **4** | PRESENT SUBJUNCTIVE | | **5** | IMPERFECT SUBJUNCTIVE |
|---|---|---|---|---|
| je | donne | | je | donnasse |
| tu | donnes | | tu | donnasses |
| il | donne | | il | donnât |
| elle | donne | | elle | donnât |
| nous | donnions | | nous | donnassions |
| vous | donniez | | vous | donnassiez |
| ils | donnent | | ils | donnassent |
| elles | donnent | | elles | donnassent |

| **6** | FUTURE | | **7** | CONDITIONAL |
|---|---|---|---|---|
| je | donnerai | | je | donnerais |
| tu | donneras | | tu | donnerais |
| il | donnera | | il | donnerait |
| elle | donnera | | elle | donnerait |
| nous | donnerons | | nous | donnerions |
| vous | donnerez | | vous | donneriez |
| ils | donneront | | ils | donneraient |
| elles | donneront | | elles | donneraient |

## Simple Tenses: Second Conjugation

● The stem is formed as follows:

| TENSE | FORMATION | EXAMPLE |
|---|---|---|
| Present | | |
| Imperfect | | |
| Past Historic | infinitive minus **-ir** | **fin-** |
| Present Subjunctive | | |
| Imperfect Subjunctive | | |
| Future | infinitive | **finir-** |
| Conditional | | |

● To the appropriate stem add the following endings:

| | | PRESENT (→**1**) | IMPERFECT (→**2**) | PAST HISTORIC (→**3**) |
|---|---|---|---|---|
| sing. | 1st person | **-is** | **-issais** | **-is** |
| | 2nd person | **-is** | **-issais** | **-is** |
| | 3rd person | **-it** | **-issait** | **-it** |
| plur. | 1st person | **-issons** | **-issions** | **-îmes** |
| | 2nd person | **-issez** | **-issiez** | **-îtes** |
| | 3rd person | **-issent** | **-issaient** | **-irent** |

| | | PRESENT SUBJUNCTIVE (→**4**) | IMPERFECT SUBJUNCTIVE (→**5**) |
|---|---|---|---|
| sing. | 1st person | **-isse** | **-isse** |
| | 2nd person | **-isses** | **-isses** |
| | 3rd person | **-isse** | **-ît** |
| plur. | 1st person | **-issions** | **-issions** |
| | 2nd person | **-issiez** | **-issiez** |
| | 3rd person | **-issent** | **-issent** |

| | | FUTURE (→**6**) | CONDITIONAL (→**7**) |
|---|---|---|---|
| sing. | 1st person | **-ai** | **-ais** |
| | 2nd person | **-as** | **-ais** |
| | 3rd person | **-a** | **-ait** |
| plur. | 1st person | **-ons** | **-ions** |
| | 2nd person | **-ez** | **-iez** |
| | 3rd person | **-ont** | **-aient** |

| **1** PRESENT | | **2** IMPERFECT | | **3** PAST HISTORIC | |
|---|---|---|---|---|---|
| je | finis | je | finissais | je | finis |
| tu | finis | tu | finissais | tu | finis |
| il | finit | il | finissait | il | finit |
| elle | finit | elle | finissait | elle | finit |
| nous | finissons | nous | finissions | nous | finîmes |
| vous | finissez | vous | finissiez | vous | finîtes |
| ils | finissent | ils | finissaient | ils | finirent |
| elles | finissent | elles | finissaient | elles | finirent |

| **4** PRESENT SUBJUNCTIVE | | **5** IMPERFECT SUBJUNCTIVE | |
|---|---|---|---|
| je | finisse | je | finisse |
| tu | finisses | tu | finisses |
| il | finisse | il | finît |
| elle | finisse | elle | finît |
| nous | finissions | nous | finissions |
| vous | finissiez | vous | finissiez |
| ils | finissent | ils | finissent |
| elles | finissent | elles | finissent |

| **6** FUTURE | | **7** CONDITIONAL | |
|---|---|---|---|
| je | finirai | je | finirais |
| tu | finiras | tu | finirais |
| il | finira | il | finirait |
| elle | finira | elle | finirait |
| nous | finirons | nous | finirions |
| vous | finirez | vous | finiriez |
| ils | finiront | ils | finiraient |
| elles | finiront | elles | finiraient |

## Simple Tenses: Third Conjugation

● The stem is formed as follows:

| TENSE | FORMATION | EXAMPLE |
|---|---|---|
| Present | | |
| Imperfect | | |
| Past Historic | infinitive minus **-re** | **vend-** |
| Present Subjunctive | | |
| Imperfect Subjunctive | | |
| Future | infinitive minus **-e** | **vendr-** |
| Conditional | | |

● To the appropriate stem add the following endings:

| | | PRESENT (→**1**) | IMPERFECT (→**2**) | PAST HISTORIC (→**3**) |
|---|---|---|---|---|
| sing. | 1st person | **-s** | **-ais** | **-is** |
| | 2nd person | **-s** | **-ais** | **-is** |
| | 3rd person | **–** | **-ait** | **-it** |
| plur. | 1st person | **-ons** | **-ions** | **-îmes** |
| | 2nd person | **-ez** | **-iez** | **-îtes** |
| | 3rd person | **-ent** | **-aient** | **-irent** |

| | | PRESENT SUBJUNCTIVE (→**4**) | IMPERFECT SUBJUNCTIVE (→**5**) |
|---|---|---|---|
| sing. | 1st person | **-e** | **-isse** |
| | 2nd person | **-es** | **-isses** |
| | 3rd person | **-e** | **-ît** |
| plur. | 1st person | **-ions** | **-issions** |
| | 2nd person | **-iez** | **-issiez** |
| | 3rd person | **-ent** | **-issent** |

| | | FUTURE (→**6**) | CONDITIONAL (→**7**) |
|---|---|---|---|
| sing. | 1st person | **-ai** | **-ais** |
| | 2nd person | **-as** | **-ais** |
| | 3rd person | **-a** | **-ait** |
| plur. | 1st person | **-ons** | **-ions** |
| | 2nd person | **-ez** | **-iez** |
| | 3rd person | **-ont** | **-aient** |

| **1** PRESENT | | **2** IMPERFECT | | **3** PAST HISTORIC | |
|---|---|---|---|---|---|
| je | vend**s** | je | vend**ais** | je | vend**is** |
| tu | vend**s** | tu | vend**ais** | tu | vend**is** |
| il | vend | il | vend**ait** | il | vend**it** |
| elle | vend | elle | vend**ait** | elle | vend**it** |
| nous | vend**ons** | nous | vend**ions** | nous | vend**îmes** |
| vous | vend**ez** | vous | vend**iez** | vous | vend**îtes** |
| ils | vend**ent** | ils | vend**aient** | ils | vend**irent** |
| elles | vend**ent** | elles | vend**aient** | elles | vend**irent** |

| **4** PRESENT SUBJUNCTIVE | | **5** IMPERFECT SUBJUNCTIVE | |
|---|---|---|---|
| je | vend**e** | je | vend**isse** |
| tu | vend**es** | tu | vend**isses** |
| il | vend**e** | il | vend**ît** |
| elle | vend**e** | elle | vend**ît** |
| nous | vend**ions** | nous | vend**issions** |
| vous | vend**iez** | vous | vend**issiez** |
| ils | vend**ent** | ils | vend**issent** |
| elles | vend**ent** | elles | vend**issent** |

| **6** FUTURE | | **7** CONDITIONAL | |
|---|---|---|---|
| je | vend**rai** | je | vend**rais** |
| tu | vend**ras** | tu | vend**rais** |
| il | vend**ra** | il | vend**rait** |
| elle | vend**ra** | elle | vend**rait** |
| nous | vend**rons** | nous | vend**rions** |
| vous | vend**rez** | vous | vend**riez** |
| ils | vend**ront** | ils | vend**raient** |
| elles | vend**ront** | elles | vend**raient** |

## First Conjugation Spelling Irregularities

Before certain endings, the stems of some '-er' verbs may change slightly.

Below, and on subsequent pages, the verb types are identified, and the changes described are illustrated by means of a representative verb.

Verbs ending:    **-cer**
Change:    **c** becomes **ç** before **a** or **o**
Tenses affected:    Present, Imperfect, Past Historic, Imperfect Subjunctive, Present Participle
Model:    **lancer** *to throw* (→ **1**)

● Why the change occurs:
A cedilla is added to the **c** to retain its soft [s] pronunciation before the vowels **a** and **o**

Verbs ending:    **-ger**
Change:    **g** becomes **ge** before **a** or **o**
Tenses affected:    Present, Imperfect, Past Historic, Imperfect Subjunctive, Present Participle
Model:    **manger** *to eat* (→ **2**)

● Why the change occurs:
An **e** is added after the **g** to retain its soft [ʒ] pronunciation before the vowels **a** and **o**

*Continued*

**1**

*INFINITIVE*
**lancer**

*PRESENT PARTICIPLE*
**lançant**

*PRESENT*
je lance
tu lances
il/elle lance
**nous lançons**
vous lancez
ils/elles lancent

*IMPERFECT*
**je lançais**
**tu lançais**
**il/elle lançait**
nous lancions
vous lanciez
**ils/elles lançaient**

*PAST HISTORIC*
**je lançai**
**tu lanças**
**il/elle lança**
**nous lançâmes**
**vous lançâtes**
ils/elles lancèrent

*IMPERFECT SUBJUNCTIVE*
**je lançasse**
**tu lançasses**
**il/elle lançât**
**nous lançassions**
**vous lançassiez**
**ils/elles lançassent**

**2**

*INFINITIVE*
**manger**

*PRESENT PARTICIPLE*
**mangeant**

*PRESENT*
je mange
tu manges
il/elle mange
**nous mangeons**
vous mangez
ils/elles mangent

*IMPERFECT*
**je mangeais**
**tu mangeais**
**il/elle mangeait**
nous mangions
vous mangiez
**ils/elles mangeaient**

*PAST HISTORIC*
**je mangeai**
**tu mangeas**
**il/elle mangea**
**nous mangeâmes**
**vous mangeâtes**
ils/elles mangèrent

*IMPERFECT SUBJUNCTIVE*
**je mangeasse**
**tu mangeasses**
**il/elle mangeât**
**nous mangeassions**
**vous mangeassiez**
**ils/elles mangeassent**

# First Conjugation Spelling Irregularities (ctd.)

Verbs ending     **-eler**
Change:     **-l** doubles before **-e**, **-es**, **-ent** and throughout the Future and Conditional tenses
Tenses affected:     Present, Present Subjunctive, Future, Conditional
Model:     **appeler** *to call* (→ **1**)

● Exceptions: **geler** *to freeze* } like **mener** (p. 18)
             **peler** *to peel*


Verbs ending     **-eter**
Change:     **-t** doubles before **-e**, **es**, **-ent** and throughout the Future and Conditional tenses
Tenses affected:     Present, Present Subjunctive, Future, Conditional
Model:     **jeter** *to throw* (→ **2**)

● Exceptions: **acheter** *to buy* } like **mener** (p. 18)
             **haleter** *to pant*


Verbs ending     **-yer**
Change:     **y** changes to **i** before **-e**, **-es**, **-ent** and throughout the Future and Conditional tenses
Tenses affected:     Present, Present Subjunctive, Future, Conditional
Model:     **essuyer** *to wipe* (→ **3**)

● The change described is optional for verbs ending in **-ayer** e.g. **payer** *to pay*, **essayer** *to try*

*Continued*

**1**   *PRESENT (+ SUBJUNCTIVE)*

         j'**appelle**
     tu **appelles**
  il/elle **appelle**
   nous appelons
       (appelions)
   vous appelez
       (appeliez)
ils/elles **appellent**

*FUTURE*

      j'**appellerai**
   tu **appelleras**
   il **appellera** *etc.*

*CONDITIONAL*

     j'**appellerais**
  tu **appellerais**
  il **appellerait** *etc.*

**2**   *PRESENT (+ SUBJUNCTIVE)*

       je **jette**
     tu **jettes**
  il/elle **jette**
   nous jetons
      (jetions)
   vous jetez
      (jetiez)
ils/elles **jettent**

*FUTURE*

  je **jetterai**
  tu **jetteras**
  il **jettera** *etc.*

*CONDITIONAL*

  je **jetterais**
  tu **jetterais**
  il **jetterait** *etc.*

**3**   *PRESENT (+ SUBJUNCTIVE)*

       j'**essuie**
     tu **essuies**
  il/elle **essuie**
   nous essuyons
      (essuyions)
   vous essuyez
      **(essuyiez)**
ils/elles **essuient**

*FUTURE*

     j'**essuierai**
   tu **essuieras**
   il **essuiera** *etc.*

*CONDITIONAL*

    j'**essuierais**
  tu **essuierais**
  il **essuierait** *etc.*

# First Conjugation Spelling Irregularities (ctd.)

| | |
|---|---|
| Verbs ending | **mener**, **peser**, **lever** etc |
| Change: | e changes to **è**, before **-e**, **-es**, **-ent** and throughout the Future and Conditional tenses |
| Tenses affected: | Present, Present Subjunctive, Future, Conditional |
| Model: | **mener** *to lead* (→ **1**) |

| | |
|---|---|
| Verbs like: | **céder**, **régler**, **espérer** etc |
| Change: | é changes to **è** before **-e**, **-es**, **-ent** |
| Tenses affected: | Present, Present Subjunctive |
| Model: | **céder** *to yield* (→ **2**) |

**1**   *PRESENT (+ SUBJUNCTIVE)*

| | |
|---:|:---|
| je | **mène** |
| tu | **mènes** |
| il/elle | **mène** |
| nous | menons |
| | (menions) |
| vous | menez |
| | (meniez) |
| ils/elles | **mènent** |

*FUTURE*

| | |
|---:|:---|
| je | **mènerai** |
| tu | **mèneras** |
| il | **mènera** *etc.* |

*CONDITIONAL*

| | |
|---:|:---|
| je | **mènerais** |
| tu | **mènerais** |
| il | **mènerait** *etc.* |

**2**   *PRESENT (+ SUBJUNCTIVE)*

| | |
|---:|:---|
| je | **cède** |
| tu | **cèdes** |
| il/elle | **cède** |
| nous | cédons |
| | (cédions) |
| vous | cédez |
| | (cédiez) |
| ils/elles | **cèdent** |

# The Imperative

The imperative is the form of the verb used to give commands or orders. It can be used politely, as in English 'Shut the door, please'.

The imperative is the same as the present tense **tu**, **nous** and **vous** forms without the subject pronouns:

| | | |
|---|---|---|
| **donne*** | **finis** | **vends** |
| *give* | *finish* | *sell* |

*The final 's' of the present tense of first conjugation verbs is dropped, except before **y** and **en** (→ **1**)

| | | |
|---|---|---|
| **donnons** | **finissons** | **vendons** |
| *let's give* | *let's finish* | *let's sell* |

| | | |
|---|---|---|
| **donnez** | **finissez** | **vendez** |
| *give* | *finish* | *sell* |

● The imperative of irregular verbs is given in the verb tables, pp. 74 ff.

● Position of object pronouns with the imperative:
  in POSITIVE commands: they follow the verb and are attached to it by hyphens (→ **2**)
  in NEGATIVE commands: they precede the verb and are not attached to it (→ **3**)

● For the order of object pronouns, see p. 170

● For reflexive verbs – e.g. **se lever** *to get up* – the object pronoun is the reflexive pronoun (→ **4**)

**1** Compare: **Tu donnes de l'argent à Paul**
You give (some) money to Paul
and: **Donne de l'argent à Paul**
Give (some) money to Paul

**2** **Excusez-moi**
Excuse me
**Crois-nous**
Believe us
**Attendons-la**
Let's wait for her/it

**Envoyons-les-leur**
Let's send them to them
**Expliquez-le-moi**
Explain it to me
**Rends-la-lui**
Give it back to him/her

**3** **Ne me dérange pas**
Don't disturb me
**Ne les négligeons pas**
Let's not neglect them
**Ne leur répondez pas**
Don't answer them

**Ne leur en parlons pas**
Let's not speak to them about it
**N'y pense plus**
Don't think about it any more
**Ne la lui rends pas**
Don't give it back to him/her

**4** **Lève-toi**
Get up
**Dépêchons-nous**
Let's hurry
**Levez-vous**
Get up

**Ne te lève pas**
Don't get up
**Ne nous affolons pas**
Let's not panic
**Ne vous levez pas**
Don't get up

## Compound Tenses: formation

In French the compound tenses are:

| | |
|---|---|
| Perfect | (→ **1**) |
| Pluperfect | (→ **2**) |
| Future Perfect | (→ **3**) |
| Conditional Perfect | (→ **4**) |
| Past Anterior | (→ **5**) |
| Perfect Subjunctive | (→ **6**) |
| Pluperfect Subjunctive | (→ **7**) |

They consist of the past participle of the verb together with an auxiliary verb. Most verbs take the auxiliary **avoir**, but some take **être** (see p. 28).

Compound tenses are formed in exactly the same way for both regular and irregular verbs, the only difference being that irregular verbs may have an irregular past participle.

## The Past Participle

For all compound tenses you need to know how to form the past participle of the verb. For regular verbs this is as follows:
● 1st conjugation: replace the **-er** of the infinitive by **-é** (→ **8**)
● 2nd conjugation: replace the **-ir** of the infinitive by **-i** (→ **9**)
● 3rd conjugation: replace the **-re** of the infinitive by **-u** (→ **10**)

● See p. 50 for agreement of past participles.

*Continued*

with **avoir**

**1 j'ai donné**
I gave, have given

**2 j'avais donné**
I had given

**3 j'aurai donné**
I shall have given

**4 j'aurais donné**
I should/would have given

**5 j'eus donné**
I had given

**6 (que) j'aie donné**
(that) I gave, have given

**7 (que) j'eusse donné**
(that) I had given

**8 donner** → **donné**
to give    given

**9 finir** → **fini**
to finish    finished

**10 vendre** → **vendu**
to sell    sold

with **être**

**je suis tombé**
I fell, have fallen

**j'étais tombé**
I had fallen

**je serai tombé**
I shall have fallen

**je serais tombé**
I should/would have fallen

**je fus tombé**
I had fallen

**(que) je sois tombé**
(that) I fell, have fallen

**(que) je fusse tombé**
(that) I had fallen

## Compound Tenses: formation (ctd.)

**Verbs taking the auxiliary avoir**

Perfect tense: the present tense of **avoir** plus the past participle (→ **1**)

Pluperfect tense: the imperfect tense of **avoir** plus the past participle (→ **2**)

Future Perfect: the future tense of **avoir** plus the past participle (→ **3**)

Conditional Perfect: the conditional of **avoir** plus the past participle (→ **4**)

Past Anterior: the past historic of **avoir** plus the past participle (→ **5**)

Perfect Subjunctive: the present subjunctive of **avoir** plus the past participle (→ **6**)

Pluperfect Subjunctive: the imperfect subjunctive of **avoir** plus the past participle (→ **7**)

● For how to form the past participle of regular verbs see p. 22. The past participle of irregular verbs is given for each verb in the verb tables, pp. 74 ff.

● The past participle must agree in number and in gender with any preceding direct object (see p. 50)

*Continued*

**1** *PERFECT*

| | |
|---|---|
| j'ai donné | nous avons donné |
| tu as donné | vous avez donné |
| il/elle a donné | ils/elles ont donné |

**2** *PLUPERFECT*

| | |
|---|---|
| j'avais donné | nous avions donné |
| tu avais donné | vous aviez donné |
| il/elle avait donné | ils/elles avaient donné |

**3** *FUTURE PERFECT*

| | |
|---|---|
| j'aurai donné | nous aurons donné |
| tu auras donné | vous aurez donné |
| il/elle aura donné | ils/elles auront donné |

**4** *CONDITIONAL PERFECT*

| | |
|---|---|
| j'aurais donné | nous aurions donné |
| tu aurais donné | vous auriez donné |
| il/elle aurait donné | ils/elles auraient donné |

**5** *PAST ANTERIOR*

| | |
|---|---|
| j'eus donné | nous eûmes donné |
| tu eus donné | vous eûtes donné |
| il/elle eut donné | ils/elles eurent donné |

**6** *PERFECT SUBJUNCTIVE*

| | |
|---|---|
| j'aie donné | nous ayons donné |
| tu aies donné | vous ayez donné |
| il/elle ait donné | ils/elles aient donné |

**7** *PLUPERFECT SUBJUNCTIVE*

| | |
|---|---|
| j'eusse donné | nous eussions donné |
| tu eusses donné | vous eussiez donné |
| il/elle eût donné | ils/elles eussent donné |

## Compound Tenses: formation (ctd.)

**Verbs taking the auxiliary être**

Perfect tense:
the present tense of **être** plus the past participle (→ **1**)

Pluperfect tense:
the imperfect tense of **être** plus the past participle (→ **2**)

Future Perfect:
the future tense of **être** plus the past participle (→ **3**)

Conditional Perfect:
the conditional of **être** plus the past participle (→ **4**)

Past Anterior:
the past historic of **être** plus the past participle (→ **5**)

Perfect Subjunctive:
the present subjunctive of **être** plus the past participle (→ **6**)

Pluperfect Subjunctive:
the imperfect subjunctive of **être** plus the past participle (→ **7**)

● For how to form the past participle of regular verbs see p. 22. The past participle of irregular verbs is given for each verb in the verb tables, pp. 74 ff.

● For agreement of past participles, see p. 50

● For a list of verbs and verb types that take the auxiliary **être**, see p. 28

Continued

**1** *PERFECT*

| | |
|---|---|
| je suis tombé(e) | nous sommes tombé(e)s |
| tu es tombé(e) | vous êtes tombé(e)(s) |
| il est tombé | ils sont tombés |
| elle est tombée | elles sont tombées |

**2** *PLUPERFECT*

| | |
|---|---|
| j'étais tombé(e) | nous étions tombé(e)s |
| tu étais tombé(e) | vous étiez tombé(e)(s) |
| il était tombé | ils étaient tombés |
| elle était tombée | elles étaient tombées |

**3** *FUTURE PERFECT*

| | |
|---|---|
| je serai tombé(e) | nous serons tombé(e)s |
| tu seras tombé(e) | vous serez tombé(e)(s) |
| il sera tombé | ils seront tombés |
| elle sera tombée | elles seront tombées |

**4** *CONDITIONAL PERFECT*

| | |
|---|---|
| je serais tombé(e) | nous serions tombé(e)s |
| tu serais tombé(e) | vous seriez tombé(e)(s) |
| il serait tombé | ils seraient tombés |
| elle serait tombée | elles seraient tombées |

**5** *PAST ANTERIOR*

| | |
|---|---|
| je fus tombé(e) | nous fûmes tombé(e)s |
| tu fus tombé(e) | vous fûtes tombé(e)(s) |
| il fut tombé | ils furent tombés |
| elle fut tombée | elles furent tombées |

**6** *PERFECT SUBJUNCTIVE*

| | |
|---|---|
| je sois tombé(e) | nous soyons tombé(e)s |
| tu sois tombé(e) | vous soyez tombé(e)(s) |
| il soit tombé | ils soient tombés |
| elle soit tombée | elles soient tombées |

**7** *PLUPERFECT SUBJUNCTIVE*

| | |
|---|---|
| je fusse tombé(e) | nous fussions tombé(e)s |
| tu fusses tombé(e) | vous fussiez tombé(e)(s) |
| il fût tombé | ils fussent tombés |
| elle fût tombée | elles fussent tombées |

## Compound Tenses (ctd.)

**The following verbs take the auxiliary être**

● Reflexive verbs (see p. 30) (→ **1**)

● The following intransitive verbs (i.e. verbs which cannot take a direct object), largely expressing motion or a change of state:

| | | | |
|---|---|---|---|
| **aller** | to go (→ **2**) | **passer** | to pass |
| **arriver** | to arrive; to happen | **rentrer** | to go back/in |
| **descendre** | to go/come down | **rester** | to stay (→ **5**) |
| **devenir** | to become | **retourner** | to go back |
| **entrer** | to go/come in | **revenir** | to come back |
| **monter** | to go/come up | **sortir** | to go/come out |
| **mourir** | to die (→ **3**) | **tomber** | to fall |
| **naître** | to be born | **venir** | to come (→ **6**) |
| **partir** | to leave (→ **4**) | | |

● Of these, the following are conjugated with **avoir** when used transitively (i.e. with a direct object):

| | |
|---|---|
| **descendre** | to bring/take down |
| **entrer** | to bring/take in |
| **monter** | to bring/take up (→ **7**) |
| **passer** | to pass; to spend (→ **8**) |
| **rentrer** | to bring/take in |
| **retourner** | to turn over |
| **sortir** | to bring/take out (→ **9**) |

● Note that the past participle must show an agreement in number and gender whenever the auxiliary is **être** EXCEPT FOR REFLEXIVE VERBS WHERE THE REFLEXIVE PRONOUN IS THE INDIRECT OBJECT (see p. 50)

1 **je me suis arrêté(e)**
I stopped
**tu t'es levé(e)**
you got up

**elle s'est trompée**
she made a mistake
**ils s'étaient battus**
they had fought (one another)

2 **elle est allée**
she went

3 **ils sont morts**
they died

4 **vous êtes partie**
you left (*addressing a female person*)
**vous êtes parties**
you left (*addressing more than one female person*)

5 **nous sommes resté(e)s**
we stayed

6 **elles étaient venues**
they [female] had come

7 **Il a monté les valises**
He's taken up the cases

8 **Nous avons passé trois semaines chez elle**
We spent three weeks at her place

9 **Avez-vous sorti la voiture?**
Have you taken the car out?

## Reflexive Verbs

A reflexive verb is one accompanied by a reflexive pronoun, e.g. **se lever** *to get up*; **se laver** *to wash (oneself)*. The pronouns are:

| PERSON | SINGULAR | PLURAL |
|--------|----------|--------|
| 1st | **me (m')** | **nous** |
| 2nd | **te (t')** | **vous** |
| 3rd | **se (s')** | **se (s')** |

The forms shown in brackets are used before a vowel, an **h** 'mute', or the pronoun **y** (→ **1**)

● In positive commands, **te** changes to **toi** (→ **2**)

● The reflexive pronoun 'reflects back' to the subject, but it is not always translated in English (→ **3**)
The plural pronouns are sometimes translated as *one another*, *each other* (the 'reciprocal' meaning) (→ **4**)
The reciprocal meaning may be emphasised by **l'un(e) l'autre (les un(e)s les autres)** (→ **5**)

● Simple tenses of reflexive verbs are conjugated in exactly the same way as those of non-reflexive verbs except that the reflexive pronoun is always used. Compound tenses are formed with the auxiliary **être**. A sample reflexive verb is conjugated in full on pp. 34 and 35.

For agreement of past participles, see p. 32

### Position of Reflexive Pronouns

● In constructions other than the imperative affirmative the pronoun comes before the verb (→ **6**)

● In the imperative affirmative, the pronoun follows the verb and is attached to it by a hyphen (→ **7**)

*Continued*

**1 Je m'ennuie**
I'm bored
**Elle s'habille**
She's getting dressed
**Ils s'y intéressent**
They are interested in it

**2 Assieds-toi**
Sit down
**Tais-toi**
Be quiet

**3 Je me prépare**
I'm getting (myself) ready
**Nous nous lavons**
We're washing (ourselves)
**Elle se lève**
She gets up

**4 Nous nous parlons**
We speak to each other
**Ils se ressemblent**
They resemble one another

**5 Ils se regardent l'un l'autre**
They are looking at each other

**6 Je me couche tôt**
I go to bed early
**Comment vous appelez-vous?**
What is your name?
**Il ne s'est pas rasé**
He hasn't shaved
**Ne te dérange pas pour nous**
Don't put yourself out on our account

**7 Dépêche-toi**
Hurry (up)
**Renseignons-nous**
Let's find out
**Asseyez-vous**
Sit down

## Reflexive Verbs (ctd.)

**Past Participle Agreement**

● In most reflexive verbs the reflexive pronoun is a DIRECT object pronoun (→ **1**)

● When a direct object accompanies the reflexive verb the pronoun is then the INDIRECT object (→ **2**)

● The past participle of a reflexive verb agrees in number and gender with a direct object which *precedes* the verb (usually, but not always, the reflexive pronoun) (→ **3**)
  The past participle does not change if the direct object follows the verb (→ **4**)

Here are some common reflexive verbs:

| | | | |
|---|---|---|---|
| **s'en aller** | to go away | **se hâter** | to hurry |
| **s'amuser** | to enjoy oneself | **se laver** | to wash (oneself) |
| **s'appeler** | to be called | **se lever** | to get up |
| **s'arrêter** | to stop | **se passer** | to happen |
| **s'asseoir** | to sit (down) | **se promener** | to go for a walk |
| **se baigner** | to go swimming | **se rappeler** | to remember |
| **se blesser** | to hurt oneself | **se ressembler** | to resemble each other |
| **se coucher** | to go to bed | **se retourner** | to turn round |
| **se demander** | to wonder | **se réveiller** | to wake up |
| **se dépêcher** | to hurry | **se sauver** | to run away |
| **se diriger** | to make one's way | **se souvenir de** | to remember |
| **s'endormir** | to fall asleep | **se taire** | to be quiet |
| **s'ennuyer** | to be/get bored | **se tromper** | to be mistaken |
| **se fâcher** | to get angry | **se trouver** | to be (situated) |
| **s'habiller** | to dress (oneself) | | |

*Continued*

1 **Je m'appelle**
  I'm called (*literally: I call myself*)
  **Asseyez-vous**
  Sit down (*literally: Seat yourself*)
  **Ils se lavent**
  They wash (themselves)

2 **Elle se lave les mains**
  She's washing her hands (*literally: She's washing to herself the hands*)
  **Je me brosse les dents**
  I brush my teeth
  **Nous nous envoyons des cadeaux à Noël**
  We send presents to each other at Christmas

3 **'Je me suis endormi' s'est-il excusé**
  'I fell asleep', he apologized
  **Pauline s'est dirigée vers la sortie**
  Pauline made her way towards the exit
  **Ils se sont levés vers dix heures**
  They got up around ten o'clock
  **Elles se sont excusées de leur erreur**
  They apologised for their mistake
  **Est-ce que tu t'es blessée, Cécile?**
  Have you hurt yourself, Cécile?

4 **Elle s'est lavé les cheveux**
  She (has) washed her hair
  **Nous nous sommes serré la main**
  We shook hands
  **Christine s'est cassé la jambe**
  Christine has broken her leg

## Reflexive Verbs (ctd.)

Conjugation of: **se laver** *to wash (oneself)*

I *SIMPLE TENSES*

*PRESENT*

| | |
|---|---|
| **je me lave** | **nous nous lavons** |
| **tu te laves** | **vous vous lavez** |
| **il/elle se lave** | **ils/elles se lavent** |

*IMPERFECT*

| | |
|---|---|
| **je me lavais** | **nous nous lavions** |
| **tu te lavais** | **vous vous laviez** |
| **il/elle se lavait** | **ils/elles se lavaient** |

*FUTURE*

| | |
|---|---|
| **je me laverai** | **nous nous laverons** |
| **tu te laveras** | **vous vous laverez** |
| **il/elle se lavera** | **ils/elles se laveront** |

*CONDITIONAL*

| | |
|---|---|
| **je me laverais** | **nous nous laverions** |
| **tu te laverais** | **vous vous laveriez** |
| **il/elle se laverait** | **ils/elles se laveraient** |

*PAST HISTORIC*

| | |
|---|---|
| **je me lavai** | **nous nous lavâmes** |
| **tu te lavas** | **vous vous lavâtes** |
| **il/elle se lava** | **ils/elles se lavèrent** |

*PRESENT SUBJUNCTIVE*

| | |
|---|---|
| **je me lave** | **nous nous lavions** |
| **tu te laves** | **vous vous laviez** |
| **il/elle se lave** | **ils/elles se lavent** |

*IMPERFECT SUBJUNCTIVE*

| | |
|---|---|
| **je me lavasse** | **nous nous lavassions** |
| **tu te lavasses** | **vous vous lavassiez** |
| **il/elle se lavât** | **ils/elles se lavassent** |

## Reflexive Verbs (ctd.)

Conjugation of: **se laver** *to wash (oneself)*

II   *COMPOUND TENSES*

*PERFECT*
**je me suis lavé(e)**
**tu t'es lavé(e)**
**il/elle s'est lavé(e)**

**nous nous sommes lavé(e)s**
**vous vous êtes lavé(e)(s)**
**ils/elles se sont lavé(e)s**

*PLUPERFECT*
**je m'étais lavé(e)**
**tu t'étais lavé(e)**
**il/elle s'était lavé(e)**

**nous nous étions lavé(e)s**
**vous vous étiez lavé(e)(s)**
**ils/elles s'étaient lavé(e)s**

*FUTURE PERFECT*
**je me serai lavé(e)**
**tu te seras lavé(e)**
**il/elle se sera lavé(e)**

**nous nous serons lavé(e)s**
**vous vous serez lavé(e)(s)**
**ils/elles se seront lavé(e)s**

*CONDITIONAL PERFECT*
**je me serais lavé(e)**
**tu te serais lavé(e)**
**il/elle se serait lavé(e)**

**nous nous serions lavé(e)s**
**vous vous seriez lavé(e)(s)**
**ils/elles se seraient lavé(e)s**

*PAST ANTERIOR*
**je me fus lavé(e)**
**tu te fus lavé(e)**
**il/elle se fut lavé(e)**

**nous nous fûmes lavé(e)s**
**vous vous fûtes lavé(e)(s)**
**ils/elles se furent lavé(e)s**

*PERFECT SUBJUNCTIVE*
**je me sois lavé(e)**
**tu te sois lavé(e)**
**il/elle se soit lavé(e)**

**nous nous soyons lavé(e)s**
**vous vous soyez lavé(e)(s)**
**ils/elles se soient lavé(e)s**

*PLUPERFECT SUBJUNCTIVE*
**je me fusse lavé(e)**
**tu te fusses lavé(e)**
**il/elle se fût lavé(e)**

**nous nous fussions lavé(e)s**
**vous vous fussiez lavé(e)(s)**
**ils/elles se fussent lavé(e)s**

## The Passive

In the passive, the subject *receives* the action (e.g. *I was hit*) as opposed to *performing* it (e.g. *I hit him*). In English the verb 'to be' is used with the past participle. In French the passive is formed in exactly the same way, i.e.:

a tense of **être** + past participle

The past participle agrees in number and gender with the subject (→1)

A sample verb is conjugated in the passive voice on pp. 38 and 39.

● The indirect object in French cannot become the subject in the passive:

in **quelqu'un m'a donné un livre** the indirect object **m'** cannot become the subject of a passive verb (unlike English: *someone gave me a book→I was given a book*)

● The passive meaning is often expressed in French by:
– **on** plus a verb in the active voice (→2)
– a reflexive verb (see p. 30) (→3)

*Continued*

1 **Philippe a été récompensé**
Phillip has been rewarded
**Cette peinture est très admirée**
This painting is greatly admired
**Ils le feront pourvu qu'ils soient payés**
They'll do it provided they're paid
**Les enfants seront félicités**
The children will be congratulated
**Cette mesure aurait été critiquée si ...**
This measure would have been criticized if ...
**Les portes avaient été fermées**
The doors had been closed

2 **On leur a envoyé une lettre**
They were sent a letter
**On nous a montré le jardin**
We were shown the garden
**On m'a dit que ...**
I was told that ...

3 **Ils se vendent 30 francs (la) pièce**
They are sold for 30 francs each
**Ce mot ne s'emploie plus**
This word is no longer used

## The Passive (ctd.)

Conjugation of: **être aimé** *to be liked*

*PRESENT*
| | |
|---|---|
| je suis aimé(e) | nous sommes aimé(e)s |
| tu es aimé(e) | vous êtes aimé(e)(s) |
| il/elle est aimé(e) | ils/elles sont aimé(e)s |

*IMPERFECT*
| | |
|---|---|
| j'étais aimé(e) | nous étions aimé(e)s |
| tu étais aimé(e) | vous étiez aimé(e)(s) |
| il/elle était aimé(e) | ils/elles étaient aimé(e)s |

*FUTURE*
| | |
|---|---|
| je serai aimé(e) | nous serons aimé(e)s |
| tu seras aimé(e) | vous serez aimé(e)(s) |
| il/elle sera aimé(e) | ils/elles seront aimé(e)s |

*CONDITIONAL*
| | |
|---|---|
| je serais aimé(e) | nous serions aimé(e)s |
| tu serais aimé(e) | vous seriez aimé(e)(s) |
| il/elle serait aimé(e) | ils/elles seraient aimé(e)s |

*PAST HISTORIC*
| | |
|---|---|
| je fus aimé(e) | nous fûmes aimé(e)s |
| tu fus aimé(e) | vous fûtes aimé(e)(s) |
| il/elle fut aimé(e) | ils/elles furent aimé(e)s |

*PRESENT SUBJUNCTIVE*
| | |
|---|---|
| je sois aimé(e) | nous soyons aimé(e)s |
| tu sois aimé(e) | vous soyez aimé(e)(s) |
| il/elle soit aimé(e) | ils/elles soient aimé(e)s |

*IMPERFECT SUBJUNCTIVE*
| | |
|---|---|
| je fusse aimé(e) | nous fussions aimé(e)s |
| tu fusses aimé(e) | vous fussiez aimé(e)(s) |
| il/elle fût aimé(e) | ils/elles fussent aimé(e)s |

## The Passive (ctd.)

Conjugation of: **être aimé** *to be liked*

*PERFECT*
**j'ai été aimé(e)**      **nous avons été aimé(e)s**
**tu as été aimé(e)**      **vous avez été aimé(e)(s)**
**il/elle a été aimé(e)**      **ils/elles ont été aimé(e)s**

*PLUPERFECT*
**j'avais été aimé(e)**      **nous avions été aimé(e)s**
**tu avais été aimé(e)**      **vous aviez été aimé(e)(s)**
**il/elle avait été aimé(e)**      **ils/elles avaient été aimé(e)s**

*FUTURE PERFECT*
**j'aurai été aimé(e)**      **nous aurons été aimé(e)s**
**tu auras été aimé(e)**      **vous aurez été aimé(e)(s)**
**il/elle aura été aimé(e)**      **ils/elles auront été aimé(e)s**

*CONDITIONAL PERFECT*
**j'aurais été aimé(e)**      **nous aurions été aimé(e)s**
**tu aurais été aimé(e)**      **vous auriez été aimé(e)(s)**
**il/elle aurait été aimé(e)**      **ils/elles auraient été aimé(e)s**

*PAST ANTERIOR*
**j'eus été aimé(e)**      **nous eûmes été aimé(e)s**
**tu eus été aimé(e)**      **vous eûtes été aimé(e)(s)**
**il/elle eut été aimé(e)**      **ils/elles eurent été aimé(e)s**

*PERFECT SUBJUNCTIVE*
**j'aie été aimé(e)**      **nous ayons été aimé(e)s**
**tu aies été aimé(e)**      **vous ayez été aimé(e)(s)**
**il/elle ait été aimé(e)**      **ils/elles aient été aimé(e)s**

*PLUPERFECT SUBJUNCTIVE*
**j'eusse été aimé(e)**      **nous eussions été aimé(e)s**
**tu eusses été aimé(e)**      **vous eussiez été aimé(e)(s)**
**il/elle eût été aimé(e)**      **ils/elles eussent été aimé(e)s**

## Impersonal Verbs

Impersonal verbs are used only in the infinitive and in the third person singular with the subject pronoun **il**, generally translated *it*.

    e.g. **il pleut**
    *it's raining*
    **il est facile de dire que ...**
    *it's easy to say that ...*

The most common impersonal verbs are:

| *INFINITIVE* | *CONSTRUCTIONS* |
|---|---|
| **s'agir** | **il s'agit de** + noun (→**1**)<br>*it's a question/matter of something,*<br>*it's about something*<br>**il s'agit de** + infinitive (→**2**)<br>*it's a question/matter of doing; somebody must do* |
| **falloir** | **il faut** + noun object (+ indirect object) (→**3**)<br>*(somebody) needs something, something is necessary (to somebody)*<br>**il faut** + infinitive (+ indirect object) (→**4**)<br>*it is necessary to do*<br>**il faut que** + subjunctive (→**5**)<br>*it is necessary to do, somebody must do* |
| **grêler** | **il grêle**<br>*it's hailing* |
| **neiger** | **il neige**<br>*it's snowing* |
| **pleuvoir** | **il pleut**<br>*it's raining* |
| **tonner** | **il tonne**<br>*it's thundering* |
| **valoir mieux** | **il vaut mieux** + infinitive (→**7**)<br>*it's better to do*<br>**il vaut mieux que** + subjunctive (→**8**)<br>*it's better to do/that somebody does* |

(grêler / neiger / pleuvoir / tonner) }(→**6**)

*Continued*

1 **Il ne s'agit pas d'argent**
It isn't a question/matter of money
**De quoi s'agit-il?**
What is it about?
**Il s'agit de la vie d'une famille au début du siècle**
It's about the life of a family at the turn of the century

2 **Il s'agit de faire vite**
We must act quickly

3 **Il faut du courage pour faire ça**
One needs courage to do that; Courage is needed to do that
**Il me faut une chaise de plus**
I need an extra chair

4 **Il faut partir**
It is necessary to leave; We/I/You must leave*
**Il me fallait prendre une décision**
I had to make a decision

5 **Il faut que vous partiez**
You have to leave/You must leave
**Il faudrait que je fasse mes valises**
I should have to/ought to pack my cases

6 **Il pleuvait à verse**
It was raining heavily/It was pouring

7 **Il vaut mieux refuser**
It's better to refuse; You/He/I had better refuse*
**Il vaudrait mieux rester**
You/We/She had better stay*

8 **Il vaudrait mieux que nous ne venions pas**
It would be better if we didn't come; We'd better not come

*The translation here obviously depends on context*

## Impersonal Verbs (ctd.)

The following verbs are also commonly used in impersonal constructions:

| INFINITIVE | CONSTRUCTIONS |
| --- | --- |
| **avoir** | **il y a** + noun (→**1**) <br> *there is/are* |
| **être** | **il est** + noun (→**2**) <br> *it is; there are* (very literary style) <br> **il est** + adjective + **de** + infinitive (→**3**) <br> *it is* |
| **faire** | **il fait** + adjective of weather (→**4**) <br> *it is* <br> **il fait** + noun depicting weather/dark/light etc. <br> *it is* (→**5**) |
| **manquer** | **il manque** + noun (+ indirect object) (→**6**) <br> *there is/are ... missing, something is missing/lacking* |
| **paraître** | **il paraît que** + subjunctive (→**7**) <br> *it seems/appears that* <br> **il paraît** + indirect object + **que** + indicative (→**8**) <br> *it seems/appears to somebody that* |
| **rester** | **il reste** + noun (+ indirect object) (→**9**) <br> *there is/are ... left, (somebody) has something left* |
| **sembler** | **il semble que** + subjunctive (→**10**) <br> *it seems/appears that* <br> **il semble** + indirect object + **que** + indicative (→**11**) <br> *it seems/appears to somebody that* |
| **suffire** | **il suffit de** + infinitive (→**12**) <br> *it is enough to do* <br> **il suffit de** + noun (→**13**) <br> *something is enough, it only takes something* |

*Continued*

1. **Il y a du pain (qui reste)**
   There is some bread (left)
   **Il n'y avait pas de lettres ce matin**
   There were no letters this morning
2. **Il est dix heures**
   It's ten o'clock
   **Il est des gens qui ...**
   There are (some) people who ...
3. **Il était inutile de protester**
   It was useless to protest
   **Il est facile de critiquer**
   Criticizing is easy
4. **Il fait beau/mauvais**
   It's lovely/horrible weather
5. **Il faisait du soleil/du vent**
   It was sunny/windy
   **Il fait jour/nuit**
   It's light/dark
6. **Il manque deux tasses**
   There are two cups missing; Two cups are missing
   **Il manquait un bouton à sa chemise**
   His shirt had a button missing
7. **Il paraît qu'ils partent demain**
   It appears they are leaving tomorrow
8. **Il nous paraît certain qu'il aura du succès**
   It seems certain to us that he'll be successful
9. **Il reste deux miches de pain**
   There are two loaves left
   **Il lui restait cinquante francs**
   He/She had fifty francs left
10. **Il semble que vous ayez raison**
    It seems that you are right
11. **Il me semblait qu'il conduisait trop vite**
    It seemed to me (that) he was driving too fast
12. **Il suffit de téléphoner pour réserver une place**
    You need only phone to reserve a seat
13. **Il suffit d'une seule erreur pour tout gâcher**
    One single error is enough to ruin everything

## The Infinitive

The infinitive is the form of the verb found in dictionary entries meaning 'to . . .', e.g. **donner** *to give*, **vivre** *to live*.

There are three main types of verbal construction involving the infinitive:

> – with no linking preposition (→**1**)
> – with the linking preposition **à** (→**2**)
>   (see also p. 64)
> – with the linking preposition **de** (→**3**)
>   (see also p. 64)

### Verbs followed by an infinitive with no linking preposition

- **devoir, pouvoir, savoir, vouloir** and **falloir** (i.e. modal auxiliary verbs: p. 52) (→**1**)
- **valoir mieux:** see Impersonal Verbs, p. 40
- verbs of seeing or hearing e.g. **voir** *to see*, **entendre** *to hear* (→**4**)
- intransitive verbs of motion e.g. **aller** *to go*, **descendre** *to come/go down* (→**5**)
- **envoyer** *to send* (→**6**)
- **faillir** (→**7**)
- **faire** (→**8**)
- **laisser** *to let, allow* (→**9**)
- The following common verbs:

| | | |
|---|---|---|
| **adorer** | *to love* | |
| **aimer** | *to like, love* | (→**10**) |
| **aimer mieux** | *to prefer* | (→**11**) |
| **compter** | *to expect* | |
| **désirer** | *to wish, want* | (→**12**) |
| **détester** | *to hate* | (→**13**) |
| **espérer** | *to hope* | (→**14**) |
| **oser** | *to dare* | (→**15**) |
| **préférer** | *to prefer* | |
| **sembler** | *to seem* | (→**16**) |
| **souhaiter** | *to wish* | |

*Continued*

1 **Voulez-vous attendre?**
  Would you like to wait?
2 **J'apprends à nager**
  I'm learning to swim
3 **Essayez de venir**
  Try to come
4 **Il nous a vus arriver**                  **On les entend chanter**
  He saw us arriving                         You can hear them singing
5 **Allez voir Nicolas**
  Go and see Nicholas
  **Descends leur demander**
  Go down and ask them
6 **Je l'ai envoyé les voir**
  I sent him to see them
7 **J'ai failli tomber**
  I almost fell
8 **Ne me faites pas rire!**
  Don't make me laugh!
  **J'ai fait réparer ma valise**
  I've had my case repaired
9 **Laissez-moi passer**
  Let me pass
10 **Il aime nous accompagner**
  He likes to come with us
11 **J'aimerais mieux le choisir moi-même**
  I'd rather choose it myself
12 **Elle ne désire pas venir**
  She doesn't wish to come
13 **Je déteste me lever le matin**
  I hate getting up in the morning
14 **Espérez-vous aller en vacances?**
  Are you hoping to go on holiday?
15 **Nous n'avons pas osé y retourner**
  We haven't dared go back
16 **Vous semblez être inquiet**
  You seem to be worried

## The Infinitive: Set Expressions

The following are set in French with the meaning shown:

| | | |
|---|---|---|
| **aller chercher** | *to go for, to go and get* | (→**1**) |
| **envoyer chercher** | *to send for* | (→**2**) |
| **entendre dire que** | *to hear it said that* | (→**3**) |
| **entendre parler de** | *to hear of/about* | (→**4**) |
| **faire entrer** | *to show in* | (→**5**) |
| **faire sortir** | *to let out* | (→**6**) |
| **faire venir** | *to send for* | (→**7**) |
| **laisser tomber** | *to drop* | (→**8**) |
| **vouloir dire** | *to mean* | (→**9**) |

### The Perfect Infinitive

● The perfect infinitive is formed using the auxiliary verb **avoir** or **être** as appropriate with the past participle of the verb (→**10**)

● The perfect infinitive is found:
– following the preposition **après** *after* (→**11**)
– following certain verbal constructions (→**12**)

1 **Va chercher tes photos**
   Go and get your photos
   **Il est allé chercher Alexandre**
   He's gone to get Alexander
2 **J'ai envoyé chercher un médecin**
   I've sent for a doctor
3 **J'ai entendu dire qu'il est malade**
   I've heard it said that he's ill
4 **Je n'ai plus entendu parler de lui**
   I didn't hear anything more (said) of him
5 **Fais entrer nos invités**
   Show our guests in
6 **J'ai fait sortir le chat**
   I've let the cat out
7 **Je vous ai fait venir parce que . . .**
   I sent for you because . . .
8 **Il a laissé tomber le vase**
   He dropped the vase
9 **Qu'est-ce que cela veut dire?**
   What does that mean?
10 **avoir fini**
   to have finished
   **être allé**                        **s'être levé**
   to have gone                    to have got up
11 **Après avoir pris cette décision, il nous a appelé**
   After making/having made that decision, he called us
   **Après être sorties, elles se sont dirigées vers le parking**
   After leaving/having left, they headed for the car park
   **Après nous être levé(e)s, nous avons lu les journaux**
   After getting up/having got up, we read the papers
12 **pardonner à qn d'avoir fait**
   to forgive sb for doing/having done
   **remercier qn d'avoir fait**
   to thank sb for doing/having done
   **regretter d'avoir fait**
   to be sorry for doing/having done

## The Present Participle

**Formation**

● 1st conjugation
  Replace the **-er** of the infinitive by **-ant** (→**1**)

  – Verbs ending in **-cer**: **c** changes to **ç** (→**2**)
  – Verbs ending in **-ger**: **g** changes to **ge** (→**3**)

● 2nd conjugation
  Replace the **-ir** of the infinitive by **-issant** (→**4**)

● 3rd conjugation
  Replace the **-re** of the infinitive by **-ant** (→**5**)

● For irregular present participles, see irregular verbs, p. 74 ff.

**Uses**

The present participle has a more restricted use in French than in English.

● Used as a verbal form, the present participle is invariable. It is found:
  – on its own, where it corresponds to the English present participle (→**6**)
  – following the preposition **en** (→**7**)
  Note, in particular, the construction:
  verb + **en** + present participle
  which is often translated by an English phrasal verb, i.e. one followed by a preposition like *to run down, to bring up* (→**8**)

● Used as an adjective, the present participle agrees in number and gender with the noun or pronoun (→**9**)

● Note, in particular, the use of **ayant** and **étant** – the present participles of the auxiliary verbs **avoir** and **être** – with a past participle (→**10**)

*Continued*

1 **donner** → **donn**ant
  to give    giving
2 **lancer** → **lanç**ant
  to throw   throwing
3 **manger** → **mange**ant
  to eat     eating
4 **finir** → **finiss**ant
  to finish  finishing
5 **vendre** → **vend**ant
  to sell    selling
6 **David, habitant près de Paris, a la possibilité de ...**
  David, living near Paris, has the opportunity of ...
  **Elle, pensant que je serais fâché, a dit '...'**
  She, thinking that I would be angry, said '...'
  **Ils m'ont suivi, criant à tue-tête**
  They followed me, shouting at the top of their voices
7 **En attendant sa sœur, Richard s'est endormi**
  While waiting for his sister, Richard fell asleep
  **Téléphone-nous en arrivant chez toi**
  Telephone us when you get home
  **En appuyant sur ce bouton, on peut ...**
  By pressing this button, you can ...
  **Il s'est blessé en essayant de sauver un chat**
  He hurt himself trying to rescue a cat
8 **sortir en courant**
  to run out (*literally: to go out running*)
  **avancer en boîtant**
  to limp along (*literally: to go forward limping*)
9 **le soleil couchant**          **une lumière éblouissante**
  the setting sun                a dazzling light
  **ils sont déroutants**         **elles étaient étonnantes**
  they are disconcerting         they were surprising
10 **Ayant mangé plus tôt, il a pu ...**
   Having eaten earlier, he was able to ...
   **Etant arrivée en retard, elle a dû ...**
   Having arrived late, she had to ...

## Past Participle Agreement

Like adjectives, a past participle must sometimes agree in number and gender with a noun or pronoun. For the rules of agreement, see below.
Example: **donné**

|  | MASCULINE | FEMININE |
|---|---|---|
| SING. | donné | donnée |
| PLUR. | donnés | données |

● When the masculine singular form already ends in **-s**, no further **s** is added in the masculine plural, e.g. **pris** *taken*

### Rules of Agreement in Compound Tenses

● When the auxiliary verb is **avoir**
The past participle remains in the masculine singular form, unless a direct object precedes the verb. The past participle then agrees in number and gender with the preceding direct object (→**1**)

● When the auxiliary verb is **être**
The past participle of a non-reflexive verb agrees in number and gender with the subject (→**2**)
The past participle of a reflexive verb agrees in number and gender with the reflexive pronoun, if the pronoun is a direct object (→**3**)
No agreement is made if the reflexive pronoun is an indirect object (→**4**)

### The Past Participle as an adjective

The past participle agrees in number and gender with the noun or pronoun (→**5**)

1 **Voici le livre que vous avez demandé**
Here's the book you asked for
**Laquelle avaient-elles choisie?**
Which one had they chosen?
**Ces amis? Je les ai rencontrés à Edimbourg**
Those friends? I met them in Edinburgh
**Il a gardé toutes les lettres qu'elle a écrites**
He has kept all the letters she wrote

2 **Est-ce que ton frère est allé à l'étranger?**
Did your brother go abroad?
**Elle était restée chez elle**
She had stayed at home
**Ils sont partis dans la matinée**
They left in the morning
**Mes cousines sont revenues hier**
My cousins came back yesterday

3 **Tu t'es rappelé d'acheter du pain, Georges?**
Did you remember to buy bread, George?
**Martine s'est demandée pourquoi il l'appelait**
Martine wondered why he was calling her
**'Lui et moi nous nous sommes cachés' a-t-elle dit**
'He and I hid,' she said
**Les vendeuses se sont mises en grève**
Shop assistants have gone on strike
**Vous vous êtes brouillés?**
Have you fallen out with each other?
**Les ouvrières s'étaient entraidées**
The workers had helped one another

4 **Elle s'est lavé les mains**
She washed her hands
**Ils se sont parlé pendant des heures**
They talked to each other for hours

5 **à un moment donné**
at a given time
**ils sont bien connus**
they are well-known

**la porte ouverte**
the open door
**elles semblent fatiguées**
they seem tired

## Modal Auxiliary Verbs

● In French, the modal auxiliary verbs are: **devoir**, **pouvoir**, **savoir**, **vouloir** and **falloir**.

● They are followed by a verb in the infinitive and have the following meanings:

**devoir**     *to have to, must* (→**1**)
               *to be due to* (→**2**)
               in the conditional/conditional perfect:
               *should/should have, ought/ought to have* (→**3**)

**pouvoir**    *to be able to, can* (→**4**)
               *to be allowed to, can, may* (→**5**)
               indicating possibility: *may/might/could* (→**6**)

**savoir**     *to know how to, can* (→**7**)

**vouloir**    *to want/wish to* (→**8**)
               *to be willing to, will* (→**9**)
               in polite phrases (→**10**)

**falloir**    *to be necessary:* see Impersonal Verbs, p. 40

1 **Je dois leur rendre visite**
   I must visit them
   **Elle a dû partir**
   She (has) had to leave
   **Il a dû regretter d'avoir parlé**
   He must have been sorry he spoke
2 **Vous devez revenir demain**
   You're due (to come) back tomorrow
   **Je devais attraper le train de neuf heures mais ...**
   I was (supposed) to catch the nine o'clock train but ...
3 **Je devrais le faire**
   I ought to do it
   **J'aurais dû m'excuser**
   I ought to have apologised
4 **Il ne peut pas lever le bras**
   He can't raise his arm
   **Pouvez-vous réparer cette montre?**
   Can you mend this watch?
5 **Puis-je les accompagner?**
   May I go with them?
6 **Il peut encore changer d'avis**
   He may change his mind yet
   **Cela pourrait être vrai**
   It could/might be true
7 **Savez-vous conduire?**
   Can you drive?
   **Je ne sais pas faire une omelette**
   I don't know how to make an omelette
8 **Elle veut rester encore un jour**
   She wants to stay another day
9 **Ils ne voulaient pas le faire**
   They wouldn't do it/They weren't willing to do it
   **Ma voiture ne veut pas démarrer**
   My car won't start
10 **Voulez-vous boire quelque chose?**
   Would you like something to drink?

## Use of Tenses

### The Present

- Unlike English, French does not distinguish between the simple present (e.g. *I smoke, he reads*, we live) and the continuous present (e.g. *I am smoking, he is reading, we are living*) (→ **1**)
- To emphasise continuity, the following constructions may be used:
  **être en train de faire**  ⎫
  **être à faire**  ⎬  *to be doing* (→ **2**)
- French uses the present tense where English uses the perfect in the following cases:
  - with certain prepositions of time – notably **depuis** *for/since* – when an action begun in the past is continued in the present (→ **3**)
    Note, however, that the perfect is used as in English when the verb is negative or the action has been completed (→ **4**)
  - in the construction **venir de faire** *to have just done* (→ **5**)

### The Future

The future is generally used as in English, but note the following:
- Immediate future time is often expressed by means of the present tense of **aller** plus an infinitive (→ **6**)
- In time clauses expressing future action, French uses the future where English uses the present (→ **7**)

### The Future Perfect

- Used as in English to mean *shall/will have done* (→ **8**)
- In time clauses expressing future action, where English uses the perfect tense (→ **9**)

*Continued*

1 **Je fume** I smoke OR I am smoking
  **Il lit** He reads OR He is reading
  **Nous habitons** We live OR We are living
2 **Il est en train de travailler**
  He's (busy) working
3 **Paul apprend à nager depuis six mois**
  Paul's been learning to swim for six months (*and still is*)
  **Je suis debout depuis sept heures**
  I've been up since seven
  **Il y a longtemps que vous attendez?**
  Have you been waiting long?
  **Voilà deux semaines que nous sommes ici**
  That's two weeks we've been here (now)
4 **Ils ne se sont pas vus depuis des mois**
  They haven't seen each other for months
  **Elle est revenue il y a un an**
  She came back a year ago
5 **Elisabeth vient de partir**
  Elizabeth has just left
6 **Tu vas tomber si tu ne fais pas attention**
  You'll fall if you're not careful
  **Il va manquer le train**
  He's going to miss the train
  **Ça va prendre une demi-heure**
  It'll take half an hour
7 **Quand il viendra vous serez en vacances**
  When he comes you'll be on holiday
  **Faites-nous savoir aussitôt qu'elle arrivera**
  Let us know as soon as she arrives
8 **J'aurai fini dans une heure**
  I shall have finished in an hour
9 **Quand tu auras lu ce roman, rends-le-moi**
  When you've read the novel, give it back to me
  **Je partirai dès que j'aurai fini**
  I'll leave as soon as I've finished

## Use of Tenses (ctd.)

**The Imperfect**
- The imperfect describes:
  - an action (or state) in the past without definite limits in time (→ **1**)
  - habitual action(s) in the past (often translated by means of *would* or *used to*) (→ **2**)
- French uses the imperfect tense where English uses the pluperfect in the following cases:
  - with certain prepositions of time – notably **depuis** *for/since* – when an action begun in the remoter past was continued in the more recent past (→ **3**)
    Note, however, that the pluperfect *is* used as in English, when the verb is negative or the action has been completed (→ **4**)
  - in the construction **venir de faire** *to have just done* (→ **5**)

**The Perfect**
- The perfect is used to recount a completed action or event in the past. Note that this corresponds to a perfect tense or a simple past tense in English (→ **6**)

**The Past Historic**
- Only ever used in *written*, *literary* French, the past historic recounts a completed action in the past, corresponding to a simple past tense in English (→ **7**)

**The Past Anterior**
This tense is used instead of the pluperfect when a verb in another part of the sentence is in the past historic. That is
- in time clauses, after conjunctions like: **quand**, **lorsque** *when*, **dès que**, **aussitôt que** *as soon as*, **après que** *after* (→ **8**)
- after **à peine** *hardly, scarcely* (→ **9**)

**The Subjunctive**
- In spoken French, the present subjunctive generally replaces the imperfect subjunctive. See also pp. 58 ff.

1 **Elle regardait par la fenêtre**
She was looking out of the window
**Il pleuvait quand je suis sorti de chez moi**
It was raining when I left the house
**Nos chambres donnaient sur la plage**
Our rooms overlooked the beach

2 **Dans sa jeunesse il se levait à l'aube**
In his youth he got up at dawn
**Nous causions des heures entières**
We would talk for hours on end
**Elle te taquinait, n'est-ce pas?**
She used to tease you, didn't she?

3 **Nous habitions à Londres depuis deux ans**
We had been living in London for two years (*and still were*)
**Il était malade depuis 1985**
He had been ill since 1985
**Il y avait assez longtemps qu'il le faisait**
He had been doing it for quite a long time

4 **Voilà un an que je ne l'avais pas vu**
I hadn't seen him for a year
**Il y avait une heure qu'elle était arrivée**
She had arrived one hour before

5 **Je venais de les rencontrer**
I had just met them

6 **Nous sommes allés au bord de la mer**
We went/have been to the seaside
**Il a refusé de nous aider**
He (has) refused to help us
**La voiture ne s'est pas arrêtée**
The car didn't stop/hasn't stopped

7 **Le roi mourut en 1592**
The king died in 1592

8 **Quand il eut fini, il se leva**
When he had finished, he got up

9 **A peine eut-il parlé qu'on frappa à la porte**
He had scarcely spoken when there was a knock at the door

# The Subjunctive: when to use it

**(For how to form the subjunctive see pp. 6 ff.)**

● After certain conjunctions
**quoique**
**bien que** } *although* (→ **1**)
**pour que**
**afin que** } *so that* (→ **2**)
**pourvu que** *provided that* (→ **3**)
**jusqu'à ce que** *until* (→ **4**)
**avant que (... ne)** *before* (→ **5**)
**à moins que (... ne)** *unless* (→ **6**)
**de peur que (... ne)**
**de crainte que (... ne)** } *for fear that, lest* (→ **7**)

Note that the **ne** following the conjunctions in examples **5** to **7** has no translation value. It is often omitted in spoken informal French.

● After the conjunctions
**de sorte que**
**de façon que** } *so that* (indicating a *purpose*) (→ **8**)
**de manière que**
When these conjunctions introduce a *result* and not a *purpose*, the subjunctive is not used (→ **9**)

● After impersonal constructions which express necessity, possibility etc
**il faut que**
**il est nécessaire que** } *it is necessary that* (→ **10**)
**il est possible que** *it is possible that* (→ **11**)
**il semble que** *it seems that* (→ **12**)
**il vaut mieux que** *it is better that* (→ **13**)
**il est dommage que** *it's a pity that* (→ **14**)

*Continued*

1 **Bien qu'il fasse beaucoup d'efforts, il est peu récompensé**
Although he makes a lot of effort, he isn't rewarded for it

2 **Demandez un reçu afin que vous puissiez être remboursé**
Ask for a receipt so that you can get a refund

3 **Nous partirons ensemble pourvu que Sylvie soit d'accord**
We'll leave together provided Sylvie agrees

4 **Reste ici jusqu'à ce que nous revenions**
Stay here until we come back

5 **Je le ferai avant que tu ne partes**
I'll do it before you leave

6 **Ce doit être Paul, à moins que je ne me trompe**
That must be Paul, unless I'm mistaken

7 **Parlez bas de peur qu'on ne vous entende**
Speak softly lest anyone hears you

8 **Retournez-vous de sorte que je vous voie**
Turn round so that I can see you

9 **Il refuse de le faire de sorte que je dois le faire moi-même**
He refuses to do it so that I have to do it myself

10 **Il faut que je vous parle immédiatement**
I must speak to you right away/It is necessary that I speak …

11 **Il est possible qu'ils aient raison**
They may be right/It's possible that they are right

12 **Il semble qu'elle ne soit pas venue**
It appears that she hasn't come

13 **Il vaut mieux que vous restiez chez vous**
It's better that you stay at home

14 **Il est dommage qu'elle ait perdu cette adresse**
It's a shame/a pity that she's lost the address

## The Subjunctive: when to use it (ctd.)

● After verbs of:
  – 'wishing'
  **vouloir que**
  **désirer que**          } *to wish that, want* (→ **1**)
  **souhaiter que**

  – 'fearing'
  **craindre que**        } *to be afraid that* (→ **2**)
  **avoir peur que**

  Note that **ne** in the first phrase of example 2 has no translation
  value. It is often omitted in spoken informal French.

  – 'ordering', 'forbidding', 'allowing'
  **ordonner que**   *to order that* (→ **3**)
  **défendre que**   *to forbid that* (→ **4**)
  **permettre que**   *to allow that* (→ **5**)

  – opinion, expressing uncertainty
  **croire que**      } *to think that* (→ **6**)
  **penser que**
  **douter que**   *to doubt that* (→ **7**)

  – emotion (e.g. regret, shame, pleasure)
  **regretter que**   *to be sorry that* (→ **8**)
  **être content/surpris** etc **que**   (→ **9**)
  *to be pleased/ surprised* etc *that*

● After a superlative (→ **10**)

● After certain adjectives expressing some sort of 'uniqueness'
  **dernier ... qui/que**   *last ... who/that*
  **premier ... qui/que**   *first ... who/that*
  **meilleur ... qui/que**   *best ... who/that*   } (→ **11**)
  **seul** } **... qui/que**   *only ... who/that*
  **unique**

*Continued*

1 **Nous voulons qu'elle soit contente**
We want her to be happy (*literally: We want that she is happy*)
**Désirez-vous que je le fasse?**
Do you want me to do it?

2 **Il craint qu'il ne soit trop tard**
He's afraid it may be too late
**Avez-vous peur qu'il ne revienne pas?**
Are you afraid that he won't come back?

3 **Il a ordonné qu'ils soient désormais à l'heure**
He has ordered that they be on time from now on

4 **Elle défend que vous disiez cela**
She forbids you to say that

5 **Permettez que nous vous aidions**
Allow us to help you

6 **Je ne pense pas qu'ils soient venus**
I don't think they came

7 **Nous doutons qu'il ait dit la vérité**
We doubt that he told the truth

8 **Je regrette que vous ne puissiez pas venir**
I'm sorry that you cannot come

9 **Je suis content que vous les aimiez**
I'm pleased that you like them

10 **la personne la plus sympathique que je connaisse**
the nicest person I know
**l'article le moins cher que j'aie jamais acheté**
the cheapest item I have ever bought

11 **Voici la dernière lettre qu'elle m'ait écrite**
This is the last letter she wrote to me
**David est la seule personne qui puisse me conseiller**
David is the only person who can advise me

## The Subjunctive: when to use it (ctd.)

● After    **si (...) que**    *however (...)*   (→ **1**)
          **qui que**      *whoever*       (→ **2**)
          **quoi que**    *whatever*     (→ **3**)

   ● After **que** in the following:
      – to form the 3rd person imperative or to express a wish (→ **4**)
      – when **que** has the meaning *if*, replacing **si** in a clause (→ **5**)
      – when **que** has the meaning *whether* (→ **6**)

● In relative clauses following certain types of indefinite and negative construction (→ **7/8**)

● In set expressions (→ **9**)

1 **si courageux qu'il soit**
however brave he may be
**si peu que ce soit**
however little it is

2 **Qui que vous soyez, allez-vous-en!**
Whoever you are, go away!

3 **Quoi que nous fassions, ...**
Whatever we do, ...

4 **Qu'il entre!**
Let him come in!
**Que cela vous serve de leçon!**
Let that be a lesson to you!

5 **S'il fait beau et que tu te sentes mieux, nous irons ...**
If it's nice and you're feeling better, we'll go ...

6 **Que tu viennes ou non, je ...**
Whether you come or not, I ...

7 **Il cherche une maison qui ait deux caves**
He's looking for a house which has two cellars
(*subjunctive used since such a house may or may not exist*)
**J'ai besoin d'un livre qui décrive l'art du mime**
I need a book which describes the art of mime
(*subjunctive used since such a book may or may not exist*)

8 **Je n'ai rencontré personne qui la connaisse**
I haven't met anyone who knows her
**Il n'y a rien qui puisse vous empêcher de ...**
There's nothing that can prevent you from ...

9 **Vive le roi!**
Long live the king!
**Que Dieu vous bénisse!**
God bless you!

## Verbs governing à and de

The following lists (pp. 64 to 72) contain common verbal constructions using the prepositions **à** and **de**

Note the following abbreviations:

| | |
|---|---|
| infin. | infinitive |
| perf. infin. | perfect infinitive* |
| **qch** | quelque chose |
| **qn** | quelqu'un |
| *sb* | somebody |
| *sth* | something |

*For formation see p. 46

| | |
|---|---|
| **accuser qn de qch/de** + perf. infin. | *to accuse sb of sth/of doing, having done* (→1) |
| **accoutumer qn à qch/à** + infin. | *to accustom sb to sth/to doing* |
| **acheter qch à qn** | *to buy sth from sb/for sb* (→2) |
| **achever de** + infin. | *to end up doing* |
| **aider qn à** + infin. | *to help sb to do* (→3) |
| **s'amuser à** + infin. | *to have fun doing* |
| **s'apercevoir de qch** | *to notice sth* (→4) |
| **apprendre qch à qn** | *to teach sb sth* |
| **apprendre à** + infin. | *to learn to do* (→5) |
| **apprendre à qn à** + infin. | *to teach sb to do* (→6) |
| **s'approcher de qn/qch** | *to approach sb/sth* (→7) |
| **arracher qch à qn** | *to snatch sth from sb* (→8) |
| **(s')arrêter de** + infin. | *to stop doing* (→9) |
| **arriver à** + infin. | *to manage to do* (→10) |
| **assister à qch** | *to attend sth, be at sth* |
| **s'attendre à** + infin. | *to expect to do* (→11) |
| **blâmer qn de qch/de** + perf. infin. | *to blame sb for sth/for having done* (→12) |
| **cacher qch à qn** | *to hide sth from sb* (→13) |
| **cesser de** + infin. | *to stop doing* (→14) |

*Continued*

1 **Il m'a accusé d'avoir menti**
He accused me of lying

2 **Marie-Christine leur a acheté deux billets**
Marie-Christine bought two tickets from/for them

3 **Aidez-moi à porter ces valises**
Help me to carry these cases

4 **Il ne s'est pas aperçu de son erreur**
He didn't notice his mistake

5 **Elle apprend à lire**
She's learning to read

6 **Je lui apprends à nager**
I'm teaching him/her to swim

7 **Elle s'est approchée de moi, en disant '...'**
She came up to me, saying '...'

8 **Le voleur lui a arraché l'argent**
The thief snatched the money from him/her

9 **Arrêtez de faire du bruit!**
Stop being (so) noisy!

10 **Je n'arrive pas à le comprendre**
I can't understand it

11 **Est-ce qu'elle s'attendait à le voir?**
Was she expecting to see him?

12 **Je ne la blâme pas de l'avoir fait**
I don't blame her for doing it

13 **Cache-les-leur!**
Hide them from them!

14 **Est-ce qu'il a cessé de pleuvoir?**
Has it stopped raining?

## Verbs governing à and de (ctd.)

| | |
|---|---|
| changer de qch | *to change sth* (→ 1) |
| se charger de qch/de + infin. | *to see to sth/undertake to do* |
| chercher à + infin. | *to try to do* |
| commander à qn de + infin. | *to order sb to do* (→ 2) |
| commencer à/de + infin. | *to begin to do* (→ 3) |
| conseiller à qn de + infin. | *to advise sb to do* (→ 4) |
| consentir à qch/à + infin. | *to agree to sth/to do* (→ 5) |
| continuer à/de + infin. | *to continue to do* |
| craindre de + infin. | *to be afraid to do/of doing* |
| décider de + infin. | *to decide to* (→ 6) |
| se décider à + infin. | *to make up one's mind to do* |
| défendre à qn de + infin. | *to forbid sb to do* (→ 7) |
| demander qch à qn | *to ask sb sth/for sth* (→ 8) |
| demander à qn de + infin. | *to ask sb to do* (→ 9) |
| se dépêcher de + infin. | *to hurry to do* |
| dépendre de qn/qch | *to depend on sb/sth* |
| déplaire à qn | *to displease sb* (→ 10) |
| désobéir à qn | *to disobey sb* (→ 11) |
| dire à qn de + infin. | *to tell sb to do* (→ 12) |
| dissuader qn de + infin. | *to dissuade sb from doing* |
| douter de qch | *to doubt sth* |
| se douter de qch | *to suspect sth* |
| s'efforcer de + infin. | *to strive to do* |
| empêcher qn de + infin. | *to prevent sb from doing* (→ 13) |
| emprunter qch à qn | *to borrow sth from sb* (→ 14) |
| encourager qn à + infin. | *to encourage sb to do* (→ 15) |
| enlever qch à qn | *to take sth away from sb* |
| enseigner qch à qn | *to teach sb sth* |
| enseigner à qn à + infin. | *to teach sb to do* |
| entreprendre de + infin. | *to undertake to do* |
| essayer de + infin. | *to try to do* (→ 16) |
| éviter de + infin. | *to avoid doing* (→ 17) |

*Continued*

1 J'ai changé d'**avis**/de **robe**
  I changed my mind/my dress
  **Il faut changer de train à Toulouse**
  You have to change trains at Toulouse

2 **Il leur a commandé de tirer**
  He ordered them to shoot

3 **Il commence à neiger**
  It's starting to snow

4 **Il leur a conseillé d'attendre**
  He advised them to wait

5 **Je n'ai pas consenti à l'aider**
  I haven't agreed to help him/her

6 **Qu'est-ce que vous avez décidé de faire?**
  What have you decided to do?

7 **Je leur ai défendu de sortir**
  I've forbidden them to go out

8 **Je lui ai demandé l'heure**
  I asked him/her the time
  **Il lui a demandé un livre**
  He asked him/her for a book

9 **Demande à Alain de le faire**
  Ask Alan to do it

10 **Leur attitude lui déplaît**
  He/She doesn't like their attitude

11 **Ils lui désobéissent souvent**
  They often disobey him/her

12 **Dites-leur de se taire**
  Tell them to be quiet

13 **Le bruit m'empêche de travailler**
  The noise is preventing me from working

14 **Puis-je vous emprunter ce stylo?**
  May I borrow this pen from you?

15 **Elle encourage ses enfants à être indépendants**
  She encourages her children to be independent

16 **Essayez d'arriver à l'heure**
  Try to arrive on time

17 **Il évite de lui parler**
  He avoids speaking to him/her

## Verbs governing à and de (ctd.)

| | |
|---|---|
| **s'excuser de qch/de** + (perf.) infin. | *to apologise for sth/for doing, having done* (→ **1**) |
| **exceller à** + infin. | *to excel at doing* |
| **se fâcher de qch** | *to be annoyed at sth* |
| **feindre de** + infin. | *to pretend to do* (→ **2**) |
| **féliciter qn de qch/de** + (perf.) infin. | *to congratulate sb on sth/on doing, having done* (→ **3**) |
| **se fier à qn** | *to trust sb* (→ **4**) |
| **finir de** + infin. | *to finish doing* (→ **5**) |
| **forcer qn à** + infin. | *to force sb to do* |
| **habituer qn à** + infin. | *to accustom sb to doing* |
| **s'habituer à** + infin. | *to get/be used to doing* (→ **6**) |
| **se hâter de** + infin. | *to hurry to do* |
| **hésiter à** + infin. | *to hesitate to do* |
| **interdire à qn de** + infin. | *to forbid sb to do* (→ **7**) |
| **s'intéresser à qn/qch/à** + infin. | *to be interested in sb/sth/in doing* (→ **8**) |
| **inviter qn à** + infin. | *to invite sb to do* (→ **9**) |
| **jouer à** (+ sports, games) | *to play* (→ **10**) |
| **jouer de** (+ musical instruments) | *to play* (→ **11**) |
| **jouir de qch** | *to enjoy sth* (→ **12**) |
| **jurer de** + infin. | *to swear to do* |
| **louer qn de qch** | *to praise sb for sth* |
| **manquer à qn** | *to be missed by sb* (→ **13**) |
| **manquer de qch** | *to lack sth* |
| **manquer de** + infin. | *to fail to do* (→ **14**) |
| **se marier à qn** | *to marry sb* |
| **se méfier de qn** | *to distrust sb* |
| **menacer de** + infin. | *to threaten to do* (→ **15**) |
| **mériter de** + infin. | *to deserve to do* (→ **16**) |
| **se mettre à** + infin. | *to begin to do* |
| **se moquer de qn/qch** | *to make fun of sb/sth* |
| **négliger de** + infin. | *to fail to do* |

*Continued*

1 **Je m'excuse d'être (arrivé) en retard**
   I apologise for being (arriving) late
2 **Elle feint de dormir**
   She's pretending to be asleep
3 **Je l'ai félicitée d'avoir gagné**
   I congratulated her on winning
4 **Je ne me fie pas à ces gens-là**
   I don't trust those people
5 **Avez-vous fini de lire ce journal?**
   Have you finished reading this newspaper?
6 **Il s'est habitué à boire moins de café**
   He got used to drinking less coffee
7 **Il a interdit aux enfants de jouer avec des allumettes**
   He's forbidden the children to play with matches
8 **Elle s'intéresse beaucoup au sport**
   She's very interested in sport
9 **Il m'a invitée à danser**
   He asked me to dance
10 **Elle joue au tennis et au hockey**
   She plays tennis and hockey
11 **Il joue du piano et de la guitare**
   He plays the piano and the guitar
12 **Il jouit d'une santé solide**
   He enjoys good health
13 **Tu manques à tes parents**
   Your parents miss you
14 **Je ne manquerai pas de le lui dire**
   I'll be sure to tell him/her about it
15 **Elle a menacé de démissionner tout de suite**
   She threatened to resign at once
16 **Ils méritent d'être promus**
   They deserve to be promoted

## Verbs governing à and de (ctd.)

| | |
|---|---|
| **nuire à qch** | *to harm sth* (→ **1**) |
| **obéir à qn** | *to obey sb* |
| **obliger qn à** + infin. | *to oblige sb to do* (→ **2**) |
| **s'occuper de qch/qn** | *to look after sth/sb* (→ **3**) |
| **offrir de** + infin. | *to offer to do* (→ **4**) |
| **omettre de** + infin. | *to fail to do* |
| **ordonner à qn de** + infin. | *to order sb to do* (→ **5**) |
| **ôter qch à qn** | *to take sth away from sb* |
| **oublier de** + infin. | *to forget to do* |
| **pardonner qch à qn** | *to forgive sb for sth* |
| **pardonner à qn de** + perf. infin. | *to forgive sb for having done* (→ **6**) |
| **parvenir à** + infin. | *to manage to do* |
| **se passer de qch** | *to do/go without sth* (→ **7**) |
| **penser à qn/qch** | *to think about sb/sth* (→ **8**) |
| **permettre qch à qn** | *to allow sb sth* |
| **permettre à qn de** + infin. | *to allow sb to do* (→ **9**) |
| **persister à** + infin. | *to persist in doing* |
| **persuader qn de** + infin. | *to persuade sb to do* (→ **10**) |
| **se plaindre de qch** | *to complain about sth* |
| **plaire à qn** | *to please sb* (→ **11**) |
| **pousser qn à** + infin. | *to urge sb to do* |
| **prendre qch à qn** | *to take sth from sb* (→ **12**) |
| **préparer qn à** + infin. | *to prepare sb to do* |
| **se préparer à** + infin. | *to get ready to do* |
| **prier qn de** + infin. | *to beg sb to do* |
| **profiter de qch/de** + infin. | *to take advantage of sth/of doing* |
| **promettre à qn de** + infin. | *to promise sb to do* (→ **13**) |
| **proposer de** + infin. | *to suggest doing* (→ **14**) |
| **punir qn de qch** | *to punish sb for sth* (→ **15**) |
| **récompenser qn de qch** | *to reward sb for sth* |
| **réfléchir à qch** | *to think about sth* |
| **refuser de** + infin. | *to refuse to do* (→ **16**) |

*Continued*

1 **Ce mode de vie va nuire à sa santé**
This lifestyle will damage her health

2 **Il les a obligés à faire la vaisselle**
He made them do the washing-up

3 **Je m'occupe de ma nièce**
I'm looking after my niece

4 **Stuart a offert de nous accompagner**
Stuart has offered to go with us

5 **Les soldats leur ont ordonné de se rendre**
The soldiers ordered them to give themselves up

6 **Est-ce que tu as pardonné à Charles de t'avoir menti?**
Have you forgiven Charles for lying to you?

7 **Nous nous sommes passés d'électricité pendant plusieurs jours**
We did without electricity for several days

8 **Je pense souvent à toi**
I often think about you

9 **Permettez-moi de continuer, s'il vous plaît**
Allow me to go on, please

10 **Elle nous a persuadés de rester**
She persuaded us to stay

11 **Est-ce que ce genre de film lui plaît?**
Does he/she like this kind of film?

12 **Je lui ai pris son baladeur**
I took his personal stereo from him

13 **Ils ont promis à Pascale de venir**
They promised Pascale that they would come

14 **J'ai proposé de les inviter**
I suggested inviting them

15 **Il a été puni de sa malhonnêteté**
He has been punished for his dishonesty

16 **Il a refusé de coopérer**
He has refused to cooperate

## Verbs governing à and de (ctd.)

| | |
|---|---|
| **regretter de** + perf. infin. | *to regret doing, having done* (→ 1) |
| **remercier qn de qch/de** + perf. infin. | *to thank sb for sth/for doing, having done* (→ 2) |
| **renoncer à qch/à** + infin. | *to give sth up/give up doing* |
| **reprocher qch à qn** | *to reproach sb with/for sth* (→ 3) |
| **résister à qch** | *to resist sth* (→ 4) |
| **résoudre de** + infin. | *to resolve to do* |
| **ressembler à qn/qch** | *to look/be like sb/sth* (→ 5) |
| **réussir à** + infin. | *to manage to do* (→ 6) |
| **rire de qn/qch** | *to laugh at sb/sth* |
| **risquer de** + infin. | *to risk doing* (→ 7) |
| **servir à qch/à** + infin. | *to be used for sth/for doing* (→ 8) |
| **se servir de qch** | *to use sth; to help oneself to sth* (→ 9) |
| **songer à** + infin. | *to think of doing* |
| **se souvenir de qn/qch/de** + perf. infin. | *to remember sb/sth/doing, having done* (→ 10) |
| **succéder à qn** | *to succeed sb* |
| **survivre à qn** | *to outlive sb* (→ 11) |
| **tâcher de** + infin. | *to try to do* (→ 12) |
| **tarder à** + infin. | *to delay doing* (→ 13) |
| **tendre à** + infin. | *to tend to do* |
| **tenir à** + infin. | *to be keen to do* (→ 14) |
| **tenter de** + infin. | *to try to do* (→ 15) |
| **se tromper de qch** | *to be wrong about sth* (→ 16) |
| **venir de\*** + infin. | *to have just done* (→ 17) |
| **vivre de qch** | *to live on sth* |
| **voler qch à qn** | *to steal sth from sb* |

*\*See also Use of Tenses, pp. 54 and 56*

1 **Je regrette de ne pas vous avoir écrit plus tôt**
I'm sorry for not writing to you sooner

2 **Nous les avons remerciés de leur gentillesse**
We thanked them for their kindness

3 **On lui reproche son manque d'enthousiasme**
They're reproaching him for his lack of enthusiasm

4 **Comment résistez-vous à la tentation?**
How do you resist temptation?

5 **Elles ressemblent beaucoup à leur mère**
They look very like their mother

6 **Vous avez réussi à me convaincre**
You've managed to convince me

7 **Vous risquez de tomber en faisant cela**
You risk falling doing that

8 **Ce bouton sert à régler le volume**
This knob is (used) for adjusting the volume

9 **Il s'est servi d'un tournevis pour l'ouvrir**
He used a screwdriver to open it

10 **Vous vous souvenez de Lucienne?**
Do you remember Lucienne?
**Il ne se souvient pas de l'avoir perdu**
He doesn't remember losing it

11 **Elle a survécu à son mari**
She outlived her husband

12 **Tâchez de ne pas être en retard!**
Try not to be late!

13 **Ils n'a pas tardé à prendre une décision**
He was not long in taking a decision

14 **Elle tient à le faire elle-même**
She's keen to do it herself

15 **J'ai tenté de la comprendre**
I've tried to understand her

16 **Je me suis trompé de route**
I took the wrong road

17 **Mon père vient de téléphoner**      **Nous venions d'arriver**
My father's just phoned      We had just arrived

## Irregular Verbs

The verbs listed opposite and conjugated on pp. 76 to 131 provide the main patterns for irregular verbs. The verbs are grouped opposite according to their infinitive ending (except **avoir** and **être**), and are shown in the following tables in alphabetical order.

In the tables, the most important irregular verbs are given in their most common simple tenses, together with the imperative and the present participle.

The auxiliary (**avoir** or **être**) is also shown for each verb, together with the past participle, to enable you to form all the compound tenses, as on pp. 24 and 26.

● For a fuller list of irregular verbs, the reader is referred to Collins Pocket French Verb Tables, which shows you how to conjugate some 2000 French verbs.

*Continued*

avoir
être

'-er':     aller
          envoyer

'-ir':     acquérir
          bouillir
          courir
          cueillir
          dormir
          fuir
          haïr
          mourir
          ouvrir
          partir
          sentir
          servir
          sortir
          tenir
          venir
          vêtir

'-oir':     s'asseoir
          devoir
          falloir
          pleuvoir
          pouvoir
          recevoir
          savoir
          valoir
          voir
          vouloir

'-re':     battre
          boire
          connaître
          coudre
          craindre
          croire
          croître
          cuire
          dire
          écrire
          faire
          lire
          mettre
          moudre
          naître
          paraître
          plaire
          prendre
          résoudre
          rire
          rompre
          suffire
          suivre
          se taire
          vaincre
          vivre

## acquérir *to acquire*    Auxiliary: avoir

**PAST PARTICIPLE**
acquis

**PRESENT PARTICIPLE**
acquérant

**IMPERATIVE**
acquiers
acquérons
acquérez

---

**PRESENT**

|  |  |
|---|---|
| j' | acquiers |
| tu | acquiers |
| il | acquiert |
| nous | acquérons |
| vous | acquérez |
| ils | acquièrent |

**FUTURE**

|  |  |
|---|---|
| j' | acquerrai |
| tu | acquerras |
| il | acquerra |
| nous | acquerrons |
| vous | acquerrez |
| ils | acquerront |

**PRESENT SUBJUNCTIVE**

|  |  |
|---|---|
| j' | acquière |
| tu | acquières |
| il | acquière |
| nous | acquérions |
| vous | acquériez |
| ils | acquièrent |

**IMPERFECT**

|  |  |
|---|---|
| j' | acquérais |
| tu | acquérais |
| il | acquérait |
| nous | acquérions |
| vous | acquériez |
| ils | acquéraient |

**CONDITIONAL**

|  |  |
|---|---|
| j' | acquerrais |
| tu | acquerrais |
| il | acquerrait |
| nous | acquerrions |
| vous | acquerriez |
| ils | acquerraient |

**PAST HISTORIC**

|  |  |
|---|---|
| j' | acquis |
| tu | acquis |
| il | acquit |
| nous | acquîmes |
| vous | acquîtes |
| ils | acquirent |

## aller *to go*

Auxiliary: **être**

*PAST PARTICIPLE*
allé

*IMPERATIVE*
**va**
allons
allez

*PRESENT PARTICIPLE*
allant

| PRESENT | | | IMPERFECT | |
|---|---|---|---|---|
| je | **vais** | | | j'allais |
| tu | **vas** | | tu | allais |
| il | **va** | | il | allait |
| nous | allons | | nous | allions |
| vous | allez | | vous | alliez |
| ils | **vont** | | ils | allaient |

| FUTURE | | | CONDITIONAL | |
|---|---|---|---|---|
| | j'**irai** | | | j'**irais** |
| tu | **iras** | | tu | **irais** |
| il | **ira** | | il | **irait** |
| nous | **irons** | | nous | **irions** |
| vous | **irez** | | vous | **iriez** |
| ils | **iront** | | ils | **iraient** |

| PRESENT SUBJUNCTIVE | | | PAST HISTORIC | |
|---|---|---|---|---|
| | j'**aille** | | | j'allai |
| tu | **ailles** | | tu | allas |
| il | **aille** | | il | alla |
| nous | allions | | nous | allâmes |
| vous | alliez | | vous | allâtes |
| ils | **aillent** | | ils | allèrent |

## s'asseoir *to sit down*　　　　Auxiliary: être

PAST PARTICIPLE
**assis**

PRESENT PARTICIPLE
**s'asseyant**

IMPERATIVE
**assieds-toi**
**asseyons-nous**
**asseyez-vous**

PRESENT
| je | m'assieds *or* assois |
| tu | t'assieds *or* assois |
| il | s'assied *or* assoit |
| nous | nous asseyons |
| | *or* assoyons |
| vous | vous asseyez *or* assoyez |
| ils | s'asseyent *or* assoient |

IMPERFECT
| je | m'asseyais |
| tu | t'asseyais |
| il | s'asseyait |
| nous | nous asseyions |
| vous | vous asseyiez |
| ils | s'asseyaient |

FUTURE
| je | m'assiérai |
| tu | t'assiéras |
| il | s'assiéra |
| nous | nous assiérons |
| vous | vous assiérez |
| ils | s'assiéront |

CONDITIONAL
| je | m'assiérais |
| tu | t'assiérais |
| il | s'assiérait |
| nous | nous assiérions |
| vous | vous assiériez |
| ils | s'assiéraient |

PRESENT SUBJUNCTIVE
| je | m'asseye |
| tu | t'asseyes |
| il | s'asseye |
| nous | nous asseyions |
| vous | vous asseyiez |
| ils | s'asseyent |

PAST HISTORIC
| je | m'assis |
| tu | t'assis |
| il | s'assit |
| nous | nous assîmes |
| vous | vous assîtes |
| ils | s'assirent |

**avoir** *to have*            Auxiliary: **avoir**

*PAST PARTICIPLE*
  **eu**

*IMPERATIVE*
  **aie**
  **ayons**
  **ayez**

*PRESENT PARTICIPLE*
  **ayant**

*PRESENT*

| | |
|---|---|
| | **j'ai** |
| tu | **as** |
| il | **a** |
| nous | **avons** |
| vous | **avez** |
| ils | **ont** |

*IMPERFECT*

| | |
|---|---|
| | **j'avais** |
| tu | **avais** |
| il | **avait** |
| nous | **avions** |
| vous | **aviez** |
| ils | **avaient** |

*FUTURE*

| | |
|---|---|
| | **j'aurai** |
| tu | **auras** |
| il | **aura** |
| nous | **aurons** |
| vous | **aurez** |
| ils | **auront** |

*CONDITIONAL*

| | |
|---|---|
| | **j'aurais** |
| tu | **aurais** |
| il | **aurait** |
| nous | **aurions** |
| vous | **auriez** |
| ils | **auraient** |

*PRESENT SUBJUNCTIVE*

| | |
|---|---|
| | **j'aie** |
| tu | **aies** |
| il | **ait** |
| nous | **ayons** |
| vous | **ayez** |
| ils | **aient** |

*PAST HISTORIC*

| | |
|---|---|
| | **j'eus** |
| tu | **eus** |
| il | **eut** |
| nous | **eûmes** |
| vous | **eûtes** |
| ils | **eurent** |

**battre** *to beat*　　　　　　　Auxiliary: **avoir**

*PAST PARTICIPLE*
battu

*IMPERATIVE*
**bats**
battons
battez

*PRESENT PARTICIPLE*
battant

| | | | |
|---|---|---|---|
| *PRESENT* | | *IMPERFECT* | |
| je | **bats** | je | battais |
| tu | **bats** | tu | battais |
| il | **bat** | il | battait |
| nous | battons | nous | battions |
| vous | battez | vous | battiez |
| ils | battent | ils | battaient |
| *FUTURE* | | *CONDITIONAL* | |
| je | battrai | je | battrais |
| tu | battras | tu | battrais |
| il | battra | il | battrait |
| nous | battrons | nous | battrions |
| vous | battrez | vous | battriez |
| ils | battront | ils | battraient |
| *PRESENT SUBJUNCTIVE* | | *PAST HISTORIC* | |
| je | batte | je | battis |
| tu | battes | tu | battis |
| il | batte | il | battit |
| nous | battions | nous | battîmes |
| vous | battiez | vous | battîtes |
| ils | battent | ils | battirent |

**boire** *to drink*        Auxiliary: **avoir**

*PAST PARTICIPLE*
  bu

*PRESENT PARTICIPLE*
  **buvant**

*IMPERATIVE*
  bois
  **buvons**
  **buvez**

| *PRESENT* | | *IMPERFECT* | |
|---|---|---|---|
| je | bois | je | **buvais** |
| tu | bois | tu | **buvais** |
| il | boit | il | **buvait** |
| nous | **buvons** | nous | **buvions** |
| vous | **buvez** | vous | **buviez** |
| ils | **boivent** | ils | **buvaient** |

| *FUTURE* | | *CONDITIONAL* | |
|---|---|---|---|
| je | boirai | je | boirais |
| tu | boiras | tu | boirais |
| il | boira | il | boirait |
| nous | boirons | nous | boirions |
| vous | boirez | vous | boiriez |
| ils | boiront | ils | boiraient |

| *PRESENT SUBJUNCTIVE* | | *PAST HISTORIC* | |
|---|---|---|---|
| je | **boive** | je | **bus** |
| tu | **boives** | tu | **bus** |
| il | **boive** | il | **but** |
| nous | **buvions** | nous | **bûmes** |
| vous | **buviez** | vous | **bûtes** |
| ils | **boivent** | ils | **burent** |

## **bouillir** *to boil*          Auxiliary: **avoir**

*PAST PARTICIPLE*
bouilli

*IMPERATIVE*
**bous**
**bouillons**
**bouillez**

*PRESENT PARTICIPLE*
**bouillant**

*PRESENT*
|       |           |
|-------|-----------|
| je    | bous      |
| tu    | bous      |
| il    | bout      |
| nous  | bouillons |
| vous  | bouillez  |
| ils   | bouillent |

*IMPERFECT*
|       |             |
|-------|-------------|
| je    | bouillais   |
| tu    | bouillais   |
| il    | bouillait   |
| nous  | bouillions  |
| vous  | bouilliez   |
| ils   | bouillaient |

*FUTURE*
|       |             |
|-------|-------------|
| je    | bouillirai  |
| tu    | bouilliras  |
| il    | bouillira   |
| nous  | bouillirons |
| vous  | bouillirez  |
| ils   | bouilliront |

*CONDITIONAL*
|       |               |
|-------|---------------|
| je    | bouillirais   |
| tu    | bouillirais   |
| il    | bouillirait   |
| nous  | bouillirions  |
| vous  | bouilliriez   |
| ils   | bouilliraient |

*PRESENT SUBJUNCTIVE*
|       |            |
|-------|------------|
| je    | bouille    |
| tu    | bouilles   |
| il    | bouille    |
| nous  | bouillions |
| vous  | bouilliez  |
| ils   | bouillent  |

*PAST HISTORIC*
|       |            |
|-------|------------|
| je    | bouillis   |
| tu    | bouillis   |
| il    | bouillit   |
| nous  | bouillîmes |
| vous  | bouillîtes |
| ils   | bouillirent |

## connaître *to know*        Auxiliary: avoir

*PAST PARTICIPLE*
**connu**

*PRESENT PARTICIPLE*
**connaissant**

*IMPERATIVE*
**connais**
**connaissons**
**connaissez**

| *PRESENT* | | *IMPERFECT* | |
|---|---|---|---|
| je | connais | je | connaissais |
| tu | connais | tu | connaissais |
| il | connaît | il | connaissait |
| nous | connaissons | nous | connaissions |
| vous | connaissez | vous | connaissiez |
| ils | connaissent | ils | connaissaient |

| *FUTURE* | | *CONDITIONAL* | |
|---|---|---|---|
| je | connaîtrai | je | connaîtrais |
| tu | connaîtras | tu | connaîtrais |
| il | connaîtra | il | connaîtrait |
| nous | connaîtrons | nous | connaîtrions |
| vous | connaîtrez | vous | connaîtriez |
| ils | connaîtront | ils | connaîtraient |

| *PRESENT SUBJUNCTIVE* | | *PAST HISTORIC* | |
|---|---|---|---|
| je | connaisse | je | connus |
| tu | connaisses | tu | connus |
| il | connaisse | il | connut |
| nous | connaissions | nous | connûmes |
| vous | connaissiez | vous | connûtes |
| ils | connaissent | ils | connurent |

## coudre *to sew*    Auxiliary: **avoir**

*PAST PARTICIPLE*
cousu

*PRESENT PARTICIPLE*
cousant

*IMPERATIVE*
couds
cousons
cousez

*PRESENT*
| je | couds |
| tu | couds |
| il | coud |
| nous | cousons |
| vous | cousez |
| ils | cousent |

*IMPERFECT*
| je | cousais |
| tu | cousais |
| il | cousait |
| nous | cousions |
| vous | cousiez |
| ils | cousaient |

*FUTURE*
| je | coudrai |
| tu | coudras |
| il | coudra |
| nous | coudrons |
| vous | coudrez |
| ils | coudront |

*CONDITIONAL*
| je | coudrais |
| tu | coudrais |
| il | coudrait |
| nous | coudrions |
| vous | coudriez |
| ils | coudraient |

*PRESENT SUBJUNCTIVE*
| je | couse |
| tu | couses |
| il | couse |
| nous | cousions |
| vous | cousiez |
| ils | cousent |

*PAST HISTORIC*
| je | cousis |
| tu | cousis |
| il | cousit |
| nous | cousîmes |
| vous | cousîtes |
| ils | cousirent |

**courir** *to run*                    Auxiliary: **avoir**

*PAST PARTICIPLE*
  couru

*PRESENT PARTICIPLE*
  courant

*IMPERATIVE*
  cours
  courons
  courez

| *PRESENT* | | *IMPERFECT* | |
|---|---|---|---|
| je | cours | je | courais |
| tu | cours | tu | courais |
| il | court | il | courait |
| nous | courons | nous | courions |
| vous | courez | vous | couriez |
| ils | courent | ils | couraient |

| *FUTURE* | | *CONDITIONAL* | |
|---|---|---|---|
| je | courrai | je | courrais |
| tu | courras | tu | courrais |
| il | courra | il | courrait |
| nous | courrons | nous | courrions |
| vous | courrez | vous | courriez |
| ils | courront | ils | courraient |

| *PRESENT SUBJUNCTIVE* | | *PAST HISTORIC* | |
|---|---|---|---|
| je | coure | je | courus |
| tu | coures | tu | courus |
| il | coure | il | courut |
| nous | courions | nous | courûmes |
| vous | couriez | vous | courûtes |
| ils | courent | ils | coururent |

## **craindre** *to fear*                    Auxiliary: **avoir**

*PAST PARTICIPLE*
**craint**

*IMPERATIVE*
**crains**
**craignons**
**craignez**

*PRESENT PARTICIPLE*
**craignant**

| *PRESENT* | | *IMPERFECT* | |
|---|---|---|---|
| je | **crains** | je | **craignais** |
| tu | **crains** | tu | **craignais** |
| il | **craint** | il | **craignait** |
| nous | **craignons** | nous | **craignions** |
| vous | **craignez** | vous | **craigniez** |
| ils | **craignent** | ils | **craignaient** |

| *FUTURE* | | *CONDITIONAL* | |
|---|---|---|---|
| je | craindrai | je | craindrais |
| tu | craindras | tu | craindrais |
| il | craindra | il | craindrait |
| nous | craindrons | nous | craindrions |
| vous | craindrez | vous | craindriez |
| ils | craindront | ils | craindraient |

| *PRESENT SUBJUNCTIVE* | | *PAST HISTORIC* | |
|---|---|---|---|
| je | **craigne** | je | **craignis** |
| tu | **craignes** | tu | **craignis** |
| il | **craigne** | il | **craignit** |
| nous | **craignions** | nous | **craignîmes** |
| vous | **craigniez** | vous | **craignîtes** |
| ils | **craignent** | ils | **craignirent** |

Verbs ending in **-eindre** and **-oindre** are conjugated similarly

**croire** *to believe*          Auxiliary: **avoir**

PAST PARTICIPLE
  **cru**

IMPERATIVE
  crois
  **croyons**
  **croyez**

PRESENT PARTICIPLE
  **croyant**

| PRESENT | | IMPERFECT | |
|---|---|---|---|
| je | crois | je | **croyais** |
| tu | crois | tu | **croyais** |
| **il** | **croit** | **il** | **croyait** |
| **nous** | **croyons** | **nous** | **croyions** |
| **vous** | **croyez** | **vous** | **croyiez** |
| ils | croient | **ils** | **croyaient** |

| FUTURE | | CONDITIONAL | |
|---|---|---|---|
| je | croirai | je | croirais |
| tu | croiras | tu | croirais |
| il | croira | il | croirait |
| nous | croirons | nous | croirions |
| vous | croirez | vous | croiriez |
| ils | croiront | ils | croiraient |

| PRESENT SUBJUNCTIVE | | PAST HISTORIC | |
|---|---|---|---|
| je | croie | **je** | **crus** |
| tu | croies | **tu** | **crus** |
| il | croie | **il** | **crut** |
| **nous** | **croyions** | **nous** | **crûmes** |
| **vous** | **croyiez** | **vous** | **crûtes** |
| ils | croient | **ils** | **crurent** |

**croître** *to grow*                    Auxiliary: **avoir**

*PAST PARTICIPLE*
**crû**

*IMPERATIVE*
**croîs**
**croissons**
**croissez**

*PRESENT PARTICIPLE*
**croissant**

*PRESENT*
| je | **croîs** |
| tu | **croîs** |
| il | **croît** |
| nous | **croissons** |
| vous | **croissez** |
| ils | **croissent** |

*IMPERFECT*
| je | **croissais** |
| tu | **croissais** |
| il | **croissait** |
| nous | **croissions** |
| vous | **croissiez** |
| ils | **croissaient** |

*FUTURE*
| je | croîtrai |
| tu | croîtras |
| il | croîtra |
| nous | croîtrons |
| vous | croîtrez |
| ils | croîtront |

*CONDITIONAL*
| je | croîtrais |
| tu | croîtrais |
| il | croîtrait |
| nous | croîtrions |
| vous | croîtriez |
| ils | croîtraient |

*PRESENT SUBJUNCTIVE*
| je | **croisse** |
| tu | **croisses** |
| il | **croisse** |
| nous | **croissions** |
| vous | **croissiez** |
| ils | **croissent** |

*PAST HISTORIC*
| je | **crûs** |
| tu | **crûs** |
| il | **crût** |
| nous | **crûmes** |
| vous | **crûtes** |
| ils | **crûrent** |

**cueillir** *to pick*                    Auxiliary: **avoir**

*PAST PARTICIPLE*
cueilli

*PRESENT PARTICIPLE*
cueillant

*IMPERATIVE*
cueille
cueillons
cueillez

*PRESENT*
| | |
|---|---|
| je | cueille |
| tu | cueilles |
| il | cueille |
| nous | cueillons |
| vous | cueillez |
| ils | cueillent |

*IMPERFECT*
| | |
|---|---|
| je | cueillais |
| tu | cueillais |
| il | cueillait |
| nous | cueillions |
| vous | cueilliez |
| ils | cueillaient |

*FUTURE*
| | |
|---|---|
| je | cueillerai |
| tu | cueilleras |
| il | cueillera |
| nous | cueillerons |
| vous | cueillerez |
| ils | cueilleront |

*CONDITIONAL*
| | |
|---|---|
| je | cueillerais |
| tu | cueillerais |
| il | cueillerait |
| nous | cueillerions |
| vous | cueilleriez |
| ils | cueilleraient |

*PRESENT SUBJUNCTIVE*
| | |
|---|---|
| je | cueille |
| tu | cueilles |
| il | cueille |
| nous | cueillions |
| vous | cueilliez |
| ils | cueillent |

*PAST HISTORIC*
| | |
|---|---|
| je | cueillis |
| tu | cueillis |
| il | cueillit |
| nous | cueillîmes |
| vous | cueillîtes |
| ils | cueillirent |

**cuire** *to cook*          Auxiliary: **avoir**

*PAST PARTICIPLE*
**cuit**

*PRESENT PARTICIPLE*
**cuisant**

*IMPERATIVE*
cuis
cuisons
cuisez

*PRESENT*

| | |
|---|---|
| je | cuis |
| tu | cuis |
| il | cuit |
| nous | cuisons |
| vous | cuisez |
| ils | cuisent |

*IMPERFECT*

| | |
|---|---|
| je | cuisais |
| tu | cuisais |
| il | cuisait |
| nous | cuisions |
| vous | cuisiez |
| ils | cuisaient |

*FUTURE*

| | |
|---|---|
| je | cuirai |
| tu | cuiras |
| il | cuira |
| nous | cuirons |
| vous | cuirez |
| ils | cuiront |

*CONDITIONAL*

| | |
|---|---|
| je | cuirais |
| tu | cuirais |
| il | cuirait |
| nous | cuirions |
| vous | cuiriez |
| ils | cuiraient |

*PRESENT SUBJUNCTIVE*

| | |
|---|---|
| je | cuise |
| tu | cuises |
| il | cuise |
| nous | cuisions |
| vous | cuisiez |
| ils | cuisent |

*PAST HISTORIC*

| | |
|---|---|
| je | cuisis |
| tu | cuisis |
| il | cuisit |
| nous | cuisîmes |
| vous | cuisîtes |
| ils | cuisirent |

**nuire** *to harm*, conjugated similarly, but past participle **nui**

**devoir** *to have to; to owe*          Auxiliary: **avoir**

PAST PARTICIPLE
**dû**

PRESENT PARTICIPLE
**devant**

IMPERATIVE
**dois**
**devons**
**devez**

PRESENT
| je | **dois** |
| tu | **dois** |
| il | **doit** |
| nous | **devons** |
| vous | **devez** |
| ils | **doivent** |

IMPERFECT
| je | **devais** |
| tu | **devais** |
| il | **devait** |
| nous | **devions** |
| vous | **deviez** |
| ils | **devaient** |

FUTURE
| je | **devrai** |
| tu | **devras** |
| il | **devra** |
| nous | **devrons** |
| vous | **devrez** |
| ils | **devront** |

CONDITIONAL
| je | **devrais** |
| tu | **devrais** |
| il | **devrait** |
| nous | **devrions** |
| vous | **devriez** |
| ils | **devraient** |

PRESENT SUBJUNCTIVE
| je | **doive** |
| tu | **doives** |
| il | **doive** |
| nous | **devions** |
| vous | **deviez** |
| ils | **doivent** |

PAST HISTORIC
| je | **dus** |
| tu | **dus** |
| il | **dut** |
| nous | **dûmes** |
| vous | **dûtes** |
| ils | **durent** |

**dire** *to say, tell*   Auxiliary: **avoir**

*PAST PARTICIPLE*
**dit**

*IMPERATIVE*
dis
disons
dites

*PRESENT PARTICIPLE*
**disant**

---

*PRESENT*
| je | dis |
| tu | dis |
| il | dit |
| nous | disons |
| vous | dites |
| ils | disent |

*IMPERFECT*
| je | disais |
| tu | disais |
| il | disait |
| nous | disions |
| vous | disiez |
| ils | disaient |

*FUTURE*
| je | dirai |
| tu | diras |
| il | dira |
| nous | dirons |
| vous | direz |
| ils | diront |

*CONDITIONAL*
| je | dirais |
| tu | dirais |
| il | dirait |
| nous | dirions |
| vous | diriez |
| ils | diraient |

*PRESENT SUBJUNCTIVE*
| je | dise |
| tu | dises |
| il | dise |
| nous | disions |
| vous | disiez |
| ils | disent |

*PAST HISTORIC*
| je | dis |
| tu | dis |
| il | dit |
| nous | dîmes |
| vous | dîtes |
| ils | dirent |

---

**interdire** *to forbid*, conjugated similarly, but 2nd person plural of the present tense is **vous interdisez**

**dormir** *to sleep*                         Auxiliary: **avoir**

*PAST PARTICIPLE*
  dormi

*IMPERATIVE*
  **dors**
  **dormons**
  **dormez**

*PRESENT PARTICIPLE*
  **dormant**

| *PRESENT* | | | *IMPERFECT* | |
|---|---|---|---|---|
| je | **dors** | | je | **dormais** |
| tu | **dors** | | tu | **dormais** |
| il | **dort** | | il | **dormait** |
| nous | **dormons** | | nous | **dormions** |
| vous | **dormez** | | vous | **dormiez** |
| ils | **dorment** | | ils | **dormaient** |

| *FUTURE* | | | *CONDITIONAL* | |
|---|---|---|---|---|
| je | dormirai | | je | dormirais |
| tu | dormiras | | tu | dormirais |
| il | dormira | | il | dormirait |
| nous | dormirons | | nous | dormirions |
| vous | dormirez | | vous | dormiriez |
| ils | dormiront | | ils | dormiraient |

| *PRESENT SUBJUNCTIVE* | | | *PAST HISTORIC* | |
|---|---|---|---|---|
| je | **dorme** | | je | dormis |
| tu | **dormes** | | tu | dormis |
| il | **dorme** | | il | dormit |
| nous | **dormions** | | nous | dormîmes |
| vous | **dormiez** | | vous | dormîtes |
| ils | **dorment** | | ils | dormirent |

## écrire *to write*    Auxiliary: avoir

PAST PARTICIPLE
**écrit**

IMPERATIVE
écris
**écrivons**
**écrivez**

PRESENT PARTICIPLE
**écrivant**

PRESENT
  j'**écris**
 tu  écris
 il  écrit
 **nous  écrivons**
 **vous  écrivez**
  **ils  écrivent**

IMPERFECT
  j'**écrivais**
  tu  **écrivais**
  il  **écrivait**
 nous  **écrivions**
 vous  **écriviez**
  ils  **écrivaient**

FUTURE
  j'**écrirai**
 tu  écriras
 il  écrira
 nous  écrirons
 vous  écrirez
  ils  écriront

CONDITIONAL
  j'**écrirais**
 tu  écrirais
 il  écrirait
 nous  écririons
 vous  écririez
  ils  écriraient

PRESENT SUBJUNCTIVE
  j'**écrive**
  tu  **écrives**
  il  **écrive**
 **nous  écrivions**
 **vous  écriviez**
  **ils  écrivent**

PAST HISTORIC
  j'**écrivis**
  tu  **écrivis**
  il  **écrivit**
 nous  **écrivîmes**
 vous  **écrivîtes**
  ils  **écrivirent**

## **envoyer** *to send*       Auxiliary: **avoir**

*PAST PARTICIPLE*
envoyé

*PRESENT PARTICIPLE*
envoyant

*IMPERATIVE*
envoie
envoyons
envoyez

| *PRESENT* | | *IMPERFECT* | |
|---|---|---|---|
| | j'envoie | | j'envoyais |
| tu | envoies | tu | envoyais |
| il | envoie | il | envoyait |
| nous | envoyons | nous | envoyions |
| vous | envoyez | vous | envoyiez |
| ils | envoient | ils | envoyaient |

| *FUTURE* | | *CONDITIONAL* | |
|---|---|---|---|
| | **j'enverrai** | | **j'enverrais** |
| **tu** | **enverras** | **tu** | **enverrais** |
| **il** | **enverra** | **il** | **enverrait** |
| **nous** | **enverrons** | **nous** | **enverrions** |
| **vous** | **enverrez** | **vous** | **enverriez** |
| **ils** | **enverront** | **ils** | **enverraient** |

| *PRESENT SUBJUNCTIVE* | | *PAST HISTORIC* | |
|---|---|---|---|
| | j'envoie | | j'envoyai |
| tu | envoies | tu | envoyas |
| il | envoie | il | envoya |
| nous | envoyions | nous | envoyâmes |
| vous | envoyiez | vous | envoyâtes |
| ils | envoient | ils | envoyèrent |

## **être** *to be*  Auxiliary: avoir

*PAST PARTICIPLE*
été

*PRESENT PARTICIPLE*
étant

*IMPERATIVE*
sois
soyons
soyez

| *PRESENT* | | *IMPERFECT* | |
|---|---|---|---|
| je | suis | | j'étais |
| tu | es | tu | étais |
| il | est | il | était |
| nous | sommes | nous | étions |
| vous | êtes | vous | étiez |
| ils | sont | ils | étaient |

| *FUTURE* | | *CONDITIONAL* | |
|---|---|---|---|
| je | serai | je | serais |
| tu | seras | tu | serais |
| il | sera | il | serait |
| nous | serons | nous | serions |
| vous | serez | vous | seriez |
| ils | seront | ils | seraient |

| *PRESENT SUBJUNCTIVE* | | *PAST HISTORIC* | |
|---|---|---|---|
| je | sois | je | fus |
| tu | sois | tu | fus |
| il | soit | il | fut |
| nous | soyons | nous | fûmes |
| vous | soyez | vous | fûtes |
| ils | soient | ils | furent |

**faire** *to do; to make*        Auxiliary: **avoir**

*PAST PARTICIPLE*
fait

*IMPERATIVE*
fais
faisons
faites

*PRESENT PARTICIPLE*
faisant

*PRESENT*
|      |         |
| ---- | ------- |
| je   | fais    |
| tu   | fais    |
| il   | fait    |
| nous | faisons |
| vous | faites  |
| ils  | font    |

*IMPERFECT*
|      |           |
| ---- | --------- |
| je   | faisais   |
| tu   | faisais   |
| il   | faisait   |
| nous | faisions  |
| vous | faisiez   |
| ils  | faisaient |

*FUTURE*
|      |        |
| ---- | ------ |
| je   | ferai  |
| tu   | feras  |
| il   | fera   |
| nous | ferons |
| vous | ferez  |
| ils  | feront |

*CONDITIONAL*
|      |          |
| ---- | -------- |
| je   | ferais   |
| tu   | ferais   |
| il   | ferait   |
| nous | ferions  |
| vous | feriez   |
| ils  | feraient |

*PRESENT SUBJUNCTIVE*
|      |          |
| ---- | -------- |
| je   | fasse    |
| tu   | fasses   |
| il   | fasse    |
| nous | fassions |
| vous | fassiez  |
| ils  | fassent  |

*PAST HISTORIC*
|      |        |
| ---- | ------ |
| je   | fis    |
| tu   | fis    |
| il   | fit    |
| nous | fîmes  |
| vous | fîtes  |
| ils  | firent |

## falloir *to be necessary*  Auxiliary: **avoir**

PAST PARTICIPLE
**fallu**

IMPERATIVE
*not used*

PRESENT PARTICIPLE
*not used*

PRESENT
il **faut**

IMPERFECT
il **fallait**

FUTURE
il **faudra**

CONDITIONAL
il **faudrait**

PRESENT SUBJUNCTIVE
il **faille**

PAST HISTORIC
il **fallut**

**fuir** *to flee* — Auxiliary: **avoir**

---

*PAST PARTICIPLE*
fui

*PRESENT PARTICIPLE*
fuyant

*IMPERATIVE*
fuis
fuyons
fuyez

---

*PRESENT*

| | |
|---|---|
| je | fuis |
| tu | fuis |
| il | fuit |
| nous | fuyons |
| vous | fuyez |
| ils | fuient |

*IMPERFECT*

| | |
|---|---|
| je | fuyais |
| tu | fuyais |
| il | fuyait |
| nous | fuyions |
| vous | fuyiez |
| ils | fuyaient |

*FUTURE*

| | |
|---|---|
| je | fuirai |
| tu | fuiras |
| il | fuira |
| nous | fuirons |
| vous | fuirez |
| ils | fuiront |

*CONDITIONAL*

| | |
|---|---|
| je | fuirais |
| tu | fuirais |
| il | fuirait |
| nous | fuirions |
| vous | fuiriez |
| ils | fuiraient |

*PRESENT SUBJUNCTIVE*

| | |
|---|---|
| je | fuie |
| tu | fuies |
| il | fuie |
| nous | fuyions |
| vous | fuyiez |
| ils | fuient |

*PAST HISTORIC*

| | |
|---|---|
| je | fuis |
| tu | fuis |
| il | fuit |
| nous | fuîmes |
| vous | fuîtes |
| ils | fuirent |

**haïr** *to hate*                    Auxiliary: avoir

PAST PARTICIPLE
haï

IMPERATIVE
hais
haïssons
haïssez

PRESENT PARTICIPLE
haïssant

PRESENT
je hais
tu hais
il hait
nous haïssons
vous haïssez
ils haïssent

IMPERFECT
je haïssais
tu haïssais
il haïssait
nous haïssions
vous haïssiez
ils haïssaient

FUTURE
je haïrai
tu haïras
il haïra
nous haïrons
vous haïrez
ils haïront

CONDITIONAL
je haïrais
tu haïrais
il haïrait
nous haïrions
vous haïriez
ils haïraient

PRESENT SUBJUNCTIVE
je haïsse
tu haïsses
il haïsse
nous haïssions
vous haïssiez
ils haïssent

PAST HISTORIC
je haïs
tu haïs
il haït
nous haïmes
vous haïtes
ils haïrent

## lire *to read*

Auxiliary: avoir

*PAST PARTICIPLE*
  lu

*IMPERATIVE*
  lis
  lisons
  lisez

*PRESENT PARTICIPLE*
  lisant

*PRESENT*
|      |        |
|------|--------|
| je   | lis    |
| tu   | lis    |
| il   | lit    |
| nous | lisons |
| vous | lisez  |
| ils  | lisent |

*IMPERFECT*
|      |          |
|------|----------|
| je   | lisais   |
| tu   | lisais   |
| il   | lisait   |
| nous | lisions  |
| vous | lisiez   |
| ils  | lisaient |

*FUTURE*
|      |        |
|------|--------|
| je   | lirai  |
| tu   | liras  |
| il   | lira   |
| nous | lirons |
| vous | lirez  |
| ils  | liront |

*CONDITIONAL*
|      |          |
|------|----------|
| je   | lirais   |
| tu   | lirais   |
| il   | lirait   |
| nous | lirions  |
| vous | liriez   |
| ils  | liraient |

*PRESENT SUBJUNCTIVE*
|      |         |
|------|---------|
| je   | lise    |
| tu   | lises   |
| il   | lise    |
| nous | lisions |
| vous | lisiez  |
| ils  | lisent  |

*PAST HISTORIC*
|      |        |
|------|--------|
| je   | lus    |
| tu   | lus    |
| il   | lut    |
| nous | lûmes  |
| vous | lûtes  |
| ils  | lurent |

**mettre** *to put*　　　　　　　　Auxiliary: **avoir**

---

PAST PARTICIPLE
mis

PRESENT PARTICIPLE
mettant

IMPERATIVE
mets
mettons
mettez

---

| PRESENT | | IMPERFECT | |
|---|---|---|---|
| je | mets | je | mettais |
| tu | mets | tu | mettais |
| il | met | il | mettait |
| nous | mettons | nous | mettions |
| vous | mettez | vous | mettiez |
| ils | mettent | ils | mettaient |

| FUTURE | | CONDITIONAL | |
|---|---|---|---|
| je | mettrai | je | mettrais |
| tu | mettras | tu | mettrais |
| il | mettra | il | mettrait |
| nous | mettrons | nous | mettrions |
| vous | mettrez | vous | mettriez |
| ils | mettront | ils | mettraient |

| PRESENT SUBJUNCTIVE | | PAST HISTORIC | |
|---|---|---|---|
| je | mette | je | mis |
| tu | mettes | tu | mis |
| il | mette | il | mit |
| nous | mettions | nous | mîmes |
| vous | mettiez | vous | mîtes |
| ils | mettent | ils | mirent |

**moudre** *to grind*            Auxiliary: **avoir**

---

*PAST PARTICIPLE*
  moulu

*PRESENT PARTICIPLE*
  moulant

*IMPERATIVE*
  mouds
  moulons
  moulez

---

*PRESENT*

| | |
|---|---|
| je | mouds |
| tu | mouds |
| il | moud |
| nous | moulons |
| vous | moulez |
| ils | moulent |

*IMPERFECT*

| | |
|---|---|
| je | moulais |
| tu | moulais |
| il | moulait |
| nous | moulions |
| vous | mouliez |
| ils | moulaient |

*FUTURE*

| | |
|---|---|
| je | moudrai |
| tu | moudras |
| il | moudra |
| nous | moudrons |
| vous | moudrez |
| ils | moudront |

*CONDITIONAL*

| | |
|---|---|
| je | moudrais |
| tu | moudrais |
| il | moudrait |
| nous | moudrions |
| vous | moudriez |
| ils | moudraient |

*PRESENT SUBJUNCTIVE*

| | |
|---|---|
| je | moule |
| tu | moules |
| il | moule |
| nous | moulions |
| vous | mouliez |
| ils | moulent |

*PAST HISTORIC*

| | |
|---|---|
| je | moulus |
| tu | moulus |
| il | moulut |
| nous | moulûmes |
| vous | moulûtes |
| ils | moulurent |

## mourir *to die*　　　　　Auxiliary: être

**PAST PARTICIPLE**
mort

**IMPERATIVE**
meurs
mourons
mourez

**PRESENT PARTICIPLE**
mourant

**PRESENT**

| | |
|---|---|
| je | meurs |
| tu | meurs |
| il | meurt |
| nous | mourons |
| vous | mourez |
| ils | meurent |

**FUTURE**

| | |
|---|---|
| je | mourrai |
| tu | mourras |
| il | mourra |
| nous | mourrons |
| vous | mourrez |
| ils | mourront |

**PRESENT SUBJUNCTIVE**

| | |
|---|---|
| je | meure |
| tu | meures |
| il | meure |
| nous | mourions |
| vous | mouriez |
| ils | meurent |

**IMPERFECT**

| | |
|---|---|
| je | mourais |
| tu | mourais |
| il | mourait |
| nous | mourions |
| vous | mouriez |
| ils | mouraient |

**CONDITIONAL**

| | |
|---|---|
| je | mourrais |
| tu | mourrais |
| il | mourrait |
| nous | mourrions |
| vous | mourriez |
| ils | mourraient |

**PAST HISTORIC**

| | |
|---|---|
| je | mourus |
| tu | mourus |
| il | mourut |
| nous | mourûmes |
| vous | mourûtes |
| ils | moururent |

**naître** *to be born*         Auxiliary: être

*PAST PARTICIPLE*
né

*PRESENT PARTICIPLE*
naissant

*IMPERATIVE*
nais
naissons
naissez

*PRESENT*

| je | nais |
|----|------|
| tu | nais |
| il | naît |
| nous | naissons |
| vous | naissez |
| ils | naissent |

*IMPERFECT*

| je | naissais |
|----|----------|
| tu | naissais |
| il | naissait |
| nous | naissions |
| vous | naissiez |
| ils | naissaient |

*FUTURE*

| je | naîtrai |
|----|---------|
| tu | naîtras |
| il | naîtra |
| nous | naîtrons |
| vous | naîtrez |
| ils | naîtront |

*CONDITIONAL*

| je | naîtrais |
|----|----------|
| tu | naîtrais |
| il | naîtrait |
| nous | naîtrions |
| vous | naîtriez |
| ils | naîtraient |

*PRESENT SUBJUNCTIVE*

| je | naisse |
|----|--------|
| tu | naisses |
| il | naisse |
| nous | naissions |
| vous | naissiez |
| ils | naissent |

*PAST HISTORIC*

| je | naquis |
|----|--------|
| tu | naquis |
| il | naquit |
| nous | naquîmes |
| vous | naquîtes |
| ils | naquirent |

**ouvrir** *to open*    Auxiliary: **avoir**

PAST PARTICIPLE
**ouvert**

IMPERATIVE
**ouvre**
**ouvrons**
**ouvrez**

PRESENT PARTICIPLE
**ouvrant**

PRESENT
|  |  |
|---|---|
|  | j'ouvre |
| tu | ouvres |
| il | ouvre |
| nous | ouvrons |
| vous | ouvrez |
| ils | ouvrent |

IMPERFECT
|  |  |
|---|---|
|  | j'ouvrais |
| tu | ouvrais |
| il | ouvrait |
| nous | ouvrions |
| vous | ouvriez |
| ils | ouvraient |

FUTURE
|  |  |
|---|---|
|  | j'ouvrirai |
| tu | ouvriras |
| il | ouvrira |
| nous | ouvrirons |
| vous | ouvrirez |
| ils | ouvriront |

CONDITIONAL
|  |  |
|---|---|
|  | j'ouvrirais |
| tu | ouvrirais |
| il | ouvrirait |
| nous | ouvririons |
| vous | ouvririez |
| ils | ouvriraient |

PRESENT SUBJUNCTIVE
|  |  |
|---|---|
|  | j'ouvre |
| tu | ouvres |
| il | ouvre |
| nous | ouvrions |
| vous | ouvriez |
| ils | ouvrent |

PAST HISTORIC
|  |  |
|---|---|
|  | j'ouvris |
| tu | ouvris |
| il | ouvrit |
| nous | ouvrîmes |
| vous | ouvrîtes |
| ils | ouvrirent |

**offrir** *to offer*, **souffrir** *to suffer* are conjugated similarly

## paraître *to appear*  Auxiliary: avoir

PAST PARTICIPLE
paru

PRESENT PARTICIPLE
paraissant

IMPERATIVE
parais
paraissons
paraissez

PRESENT
| je | parais |
| tu | parais |
| il | paraît |
| nous | paraissons |
| vous | paraissez |
| ils | paraissent |

IMPERFECT
| je | paraissais |
| tu | paraissais |
| il | paraissait |
| nous | paraissions |
| vous | paraissiez |
| ils | paraissaient |

FUTURE
| je | paraîtrai |
| tu | paraîtras |
| il | paraîtra |
| nous | paraîtrons |
| vous | paraîtrez |
| ils | paraîtront |

CONDITIONAL
| je | paraîtrais |
| tu | paraîtrais |
| il | paraîtrait |
| nous | paraîtrions |
| vous | paraîtriez |
| ils | paraîtraient |

PRESENT SUBJUNCTIVE
| je | paraisse |
| tu | paraisses |
| il | paraisse |
| nous | paraissions |
| vous | paraissiez |
| ils | paraissent |

PAST HISTORIC
| je | parus |
| tu | parus |
| il | parut |
| nous | parûmes |
| vous | parûtes |
| ils | parurent |

## partir *to leave*  Auxiliary: être

PAST PARTICIPLE
parti

PRESENT PARTICIPLE
partant

IMPERATIVE
pars
partons
partez

| PRESENT | | IMPERFECT | |
|---|---|---|---|
| je | pars | je | partais |
| tu | pars | tu | partais |
| il | part | il | partait |
| nous | partons | nous | partions |
| vous | partez | vous | partiez |
| ils | partent | ils | partaient |

| FUTURE | | CONDITIONAL | |
|---|---|---|---|
| je | partirai | je | partirais |
| tu | partiras | tu | partirais |
| il | partira | il | partirait |
| nous | partirons | nous | partirions |
| vous | partirez | vous | partiriez |
| ils | partiront | ils | partiraient |

| PRESENT SUBJUNCTIVE | | PAST HISTORIC | |
|---|---|---|---|
| je | parte | je | partis |
| tu | partes | tu | partis |
| il | parte | il | partit |
| nous | partions | nous | partîmes |
| vous | partiez | vous | partîtes |
| ils | partent | ils | partirent |

## **plaire** *to please*            Auxiliary: **avoir**

*PAST PARTICIPLE*
plu

*PRESENT PARTICIPLE*
plaisant

*IMPERATIVE*
plais
plaisons
plaisez

| *PRESENT* | | *IMPERFECT* | |
|---|---|---|---|
| je | plais | je | plaisais |
| tu | plais | tu | plaisais |
| il | plaît | il | plaisait |
| nous | plaisons | nous | plaisions |
| vous | plaisez | vous | plaisiez |
| ils | plaisent | ils | plaisaient |

| *FUTURE* | | *CONDITIONAL* | |
|---|---|---|---|
| je | plairai | je | plairais |
| tu | plairas | tu | plairais |
| il | plaira | il | plairait |
| nous | plairons | nous | plairions |
| vous | plairez | vous | plairiez |
| ils | plairont | ils | plairaient |

| *PRESENT SUBJUNCTIVE* | | *PAST HISTORIC* | |
|---|---|---|---|
| je | plaise | je | plus |
| tu | plaises | tu | plus |
| il | plaise | il | plut |
| nous | plaisions | nous | plûmes |
| vous | plaisiez | vous | plûtes |
| ils | plaisent | ils | plurent |

**pleuvoir** *to rain*      Auxiliary: **avoir**

---

*PAST PARTICIPLE*
**plu**

*IMPERATIVE*
*not used*

*PRESENT PARTICIPLE*
**pleuvant**

---

*PRESENT*
  **il pleut**

*IMPERFECT*
  **il pleuvait**

*FUTURE*
  **il pleuvra**

*CONDITIONAL*
  **il pleuvrait**

*PRESENT SUBJUNCTIVE*
  **il pleuve**

*PAST HISTORIC*
  **il plut**

**pouvoir** *to be able to*          Auxiliary: **avoir**

*PAST PARTICIPLE*
 pu

*IMPERATIVE*
 *not used*

*PRESENT PARTICIPLE*
 **pouvant**

| *PRESENT* | | *IMPERFECT* | |
|---|---|---|---|
| je | peux* | je | pouvais |
| tu | peux | tu | pouvais |
| il | peut | il | pouvait |
| nous | pouvons | nous | pouvions |
| vous | pouvez | vous | pouviez |
| ils | peuvent | ils | pouvaient |

| *FUTURE* | | *CONDITIONAL* | |
|---|---|---|---|
| je | pourrai | je | pourrais |
| tu | pourras | tu | pourrais |
| il | pourra | il | pourrait |
| nous | pourrons | nous | pourrions |
| vous | pourrez | vous | pourriez |
| ils | pourront | ils | pourraient |

| *PRESENT SUBJUNCTIVE* | | *PAST HISTORIC* | |
|---|---|---|---|
| je | puisse | je | pus |
| tu | puisses | tu | pus |
| il | puisse | il | put |
| nous | puissions | nous | pûmes |
| vous | puissiez | vous | pûtes |
| ils | puissent | ils | purent |

*In questions: **puis-je?**

**prendre** *to take*  Auxiliary: **avoir**

---

*PAST PARTICIPLE*
pris

*PRESENT PARTICIPLE*
prenant

*IMPERATIVE*
prends
prenons
prenez

---

| *PRESENT* | |
|---|---|
| je | prends |
| tu | prends |
| il | prend |
| nous | prenons |
| vous | prenez |
| ils | prennent |

| *IMPERFECT* | |
|---|---|
| je | prenais |
| tu | prenais |
| il | prenait |
| nous | prenions |
| vous | preniez |
| ils | prenaient |

| *FUTURE* | |
|---|---|
| je | prendrai |
| tu | prendras |
| il | prendra |
| nous | prendrons |
| vous | prendrez |
| ils | prendront |

| *CONDITIONAL* | |
|---|---|
| je | prendrais |
| tu | prendrais |
| il | prendrait |
| nous | prendrions |
| vous | prendriez |
| ils | prendraient |

| *PRESENT SUBJUNCTIVE* | |
|---|---|
| je | prenne |
| tu | prennes |
| il | prenne |
| nous | prenions |
| vous | preniez |
| ils | prennent |

| *PAST HISTORIC* | |
|---|---|
| je | pris |
| tu | pris |
| il | prit |
| nous | prîmes |
| vous | prîtes |
| ils | prirent |

## recevoir *to receive*      Auxiliary: **avoir**

| *PAST PARTICIPLE* | *IMPERATIVE* |
|---|---|
| reçu | reçois |
| | recevons |
| *PRESENT PARTICIPLE* | recevez |
| recevant | |

| *PRESENT* | | *IMPERFECT* | |
|---|---|---|---|
| je | reçois | je | recevais |
| tu | reçois | tu | recevais |
| il | reçoit | il | recevait |
| nous | recevons | nous | recevions |
| vous | recevez | vous | receviez |
| ils | reçoivent | ils | recevaient |

| *FUTURE* | | *CONDITIONAL* | |
|---|---|---|---|
| je | recevrai | je | recevrais |
| tu | recevras | tu | recevrais |
| il | recevra | il | recevrait |
| nous | recevrons | nous | recevrions |
| vous | recevrez | vous | recevriez |
| ils | recevront | ils | recevraient |

| *PRESENT SUBJUNCTIVE* | | *PAST HISTORIC* | |
|---|---|---|---|
| je | reçoive | je | reçus |
| tu | reçoives | tu | reçus |
| il | reçoive | il | reçut |
| nous | recevions | nous | reçûmes |
| vous | receviez | vous | reçûtes |
| ils | reçoivent | ils | reçurent |

## résoudre *to solve*　　　　Auxiliary: **avoir**

*PAST PARTICIPLE*
**résolu**

*PRESENT PARTICIPLE*
**résolvant**

*IMPERATIVE*
**résous**
**résolvons**
**résolvez**

| *PRESENT* | | *IMPERFECT* | |
|---|---|---|---|
| je | résous | je | résolvais |
| tu | résous | tu | résolvais |
| il | résout | il | résolvait |
| nous | résolvons | nous | résolvions |
| vous | résolvez | vous | résolviez |
| ils | résolvent | ils | résolvaient |

| *FUTURE* | | *CONDITIONAL* | |
|---|---|---|---|
| je | résoudrai | je | résoudrais |
| tu | résoudras | tu | résoudrais |
| il | résoudra | il | résoudrait |
| nous | résoudrons | nous | résoudrions |
| vous | résoudrez | vous | résoudriez |
| ils | résoudront | ils | résoudraient |

| *PRESENT SUBJUNCTIVE* | | *PAST HISTORIC* | |
|---|---|---|---|
| je | résolve | je | résolus |
| tu | résolves | tu | résolus |
| il | résolve | il | résolut |
| nous | résolvions | nous | résolûmes |
| vous | résolviez | vous | résolûtes |
| ils | résolvent | ils | résolurent |

**rire** *to laugh*        Auxiliary: **avoir**

*PAST PARTICIPLE*
ri

*PRESENT PARTICIPLE*
riant

*IMPERATIVE*
ris
rions
riez

| *PRESENT* | | *IMPERFECT* | |
|---|---|---|---|
| je | ris | je | riais |
| tu | ris | tu | riais |
| il | rit | il | riait |
| nous | rions | nous | riions |
| vous | riez | vous | riiez |
| ils | rient | ils | riaient |

| *FUTURE* | | *CONDITIONAL* | |
|---|---|---|---|
| je | rirai | je | rirais |
| tu | riras | tu | rirais |
| il | rira | il | rirait |
| nous | rirons | nous | ririons |
| vous | rirez | vous | ririez |
| ils | riront | ils | riraient |

| *PRESENT SUBJUNCTIVE* | | *PAST HISTORIC* | |
|---|---|---|---|
| je | rie | je | ris |
| tu | ries | tu | ris |
| il | rie | il | rit |
| nous | riions | nous | rîmes |
| vous | riiez | vous | rîtes |
| ils | rient | ils | rirent |

**rompre** *to break*      Auxiliary: **avoir**

*PAST PARTICIPLE*
rompu

*IMPERATIVE*
romps
rompons
rompez

*PRESENT PARTICIPLE*
rompant

*PRESENT*

| | |
|---|---|
| je | romps |
| tu | romps |
| il | **rompt** |
| nous | rompons |
| vous | rompez |
| ils | rompent |

*IMPERFECT*

| | |
|---|---|
| je | rompais |
| tu | rompais |
| il | rompait |
| nous | rompions |
| vous | rompiez |
| ils | rompaient |

*FUTURE*

| | |
|---|---|
| je | romprai |
| tu | rompras |
| il | rompra |
| nous | romprons |
| vous | romprez |
| ils | rompront |

*CONDITIONAL*

| | |
|---|---|
| je | romprais |
| tu | romprais |
| il | romprait |
| nous | romprions |
| vous | rompriez |
| ils | rompraient |

*PRESENT SUBJUNCTIVE*

| | |
|---|---|
| je | rompe |
| tu | rompes |
| il | rompe |
| nous | rompions |
| vous | rompiez |
| ils | rompent |

*PAST HISTORIC*

| | |
|---|---|
| je | rompis |
| tu | rompis |
| il | rompit |
| nous | rompîmes |
| vous | rompîtes |
| ils | rompirent |

## savoir *to know*

Auxiliary: **avoir**

*PAST PARTICIPLE*
  **su**

*IMPERATIVE*
**sache**
**sachons**
**sachez**

*PRESENT PARTICIPLE*
  **sachant**

*PRESENT*
|       |         |
|-------|---------|
| je    | sais    |
| tu    | sais    |
| il    | sait    |
| nous  | savons  |
| vous  | savez   |
| ils   | savent  |

*IMPERFECT*
|       |          |
|-------|----------|
| je    | savais   |
| tu    | savais   |
| il    | savait   |
| nous  | savions  |
| vous  | saviez   |
| ils   | savaient |

*FUTURE*
|       |          |
|-------|----------|
| je    | saurai   |
| tu    | sauras   |
| il    | saura    |
| nous  | saurons  |
| vous  | saurez   |
| ils   | sauront  |

*CONDITIONAL*
|       |           |
|-------|-----------|
| je    | saurais   |
| tu    | saurais   |
| il    | saurait   |
| nous  | saurions  |
| vous  | sauriez   |
| ils   | sauraient |

*PRESENT SUBJUNCTIVE*
|       |          |
|-------|----------|
| je    | sache    |
| tu    | saches   |
| il    | sache    |
| nous  | sachions |
| vous  | sachiez  |
| ils   | sachent  |

*PAST HISTORIC*
|       |        |
|-------|--------|
| je    | sus    |
| tu    | sus    |
| il    | sut    |
| nous  | sûmes  |
| vous  | sûtes  |
| ils   | surent |

**sentir** _to feel; to smell_    Auxiliary: **avoir**

PAST PARTICIPLE
 senti

PRESENT PARTICIPLE
 **sentant**

IMPERATIVE
 **sens**
 **sentons**
 **sentez**

| | PRESENT | | IMPERFECT |
|---|---|---|---|
| je | sens | je | sentais |
| tu | sens | tu | sentais |
| il | sent | il | sentait |
| nous | sentons | nous | sentions |
| vous | sentez | vous | sentiez |
| ils | sentent | ils | sentaient |

| | FUTURE | | CONDITIONAL |
|---|---|---|---|
| je | sentirai | je | sentirais |
| tu | sentiras | tu | sentirais |
| il | sentira | il | sentirait |
| nous | sentirons | nous | sentirions |
| vous | sentirez | vous | sentiriez |
| ils | sentiront | ils | sentiraient |

| | PRESENT SUBJUNCTIVE | | PAST HISTORIC |
|---|---|---|---|
| je | sente | je | sentis |
| tu | sentes | tu | sentis |
| il | sente | il | sentit |
| nous | sentions | nous | sentîmes |
| vous | sentiez | vous | sentîtes |
| ils | sentent | ils | sentirent |

**servir** *to serve*        Auxiliary: **avoir**

*PAST PARTICIPLE*
servi

*PRESENT PARTICIPLE*
**servant**

*IMPERATIVE*
**sers**
**servons**
**servez**

| *PRESENT* | | *IMPERFECT* | |
|---|---|---|---|
| je | sers | je | servais |
| tu | sers | tu | servais |
| il | sert | il | servait |
| nous | servons | nous | servions |
| vous | servez | vous | serviez |
| ils | servent | ils | servaient |

| *FUTURE* | | *CONDITIONAL* | |
|---|---|---|---|
| je | servirai | je | servirais |
| tu | serviras | tu | servirais |
| il | servira | il | servirait |
| nous | servirons | nous | servirions |
| vous | servirez | vous | serviriez |
| ils | serviront | ils | serviraient |

| *PRESENT SUBJUNCTIVE* | | *PAST HISTORIC* | |
|---|---|---|---|
| je | serve | je | servis |
| tu | serves | tu | servis |
| il | serve | il | servit |
| nous | servions | nous | servîmes |
| vous | serviez | vous | servîtes |
| ils | servent | ils | servirent |

**sortir** *to go/come out*      Auxiliary: **être**

*PAST PARTICIPLE*
sorti

*IMPERATIVE*
**sors**
**sortons**
**sortez**

*PRESENT PARTICIPLE*
**sortant**

| *PRESENT* | | | *IMPERFECT* | |
|---|---|---|---|---|
| je | **sors** | | je | **sortais** |
| tu | **sors** | | tu | **sortais** |
| il | **sort** | | il | **sortait** |
| nous | **sortons** | | nous | **sortions** |
| vous | **sortez** | | vous | **sortiez** |
| ils | **sortent** | | ils | **sortaient** |

| *FUTURE* | | | *CONDITIONAL* | |
|---|---|---|---|---|
| je | **sortirai** | | je | **sortirais** |
| tu | **sortiras** | | tu | **sortirais** |
| il | **sortira** | | il | **sortirait** |
| nous | **sortirons** | | nous | **sortirions** |
| vous | **sortirez** | | vous | **sortiriez** |
| ils | **sortiront** | | ils | **sortiraient** |

| *PRESENT SUBJUNCTIVE* | | | *PAST HISTORIC* | |
|---|---|---|---|---|
| je | **sorte** | | je | **sortis** |
| tu | **sortes** | | tu | **sortis** |
| il | **sorte** | | il | **sortit** |
| nous | **sortions** | | nous | **sortîmes** |
| vous | **sortiez** | | vous | **sortîtes** |
| ils | **sortent** | | ils | **sortirent** |

**suffire** *to be enough*          Auxiliary: avoir

*PAST PARTICIPLE*
suffi

*IMPERATIVE*
suffis
suffisons
suffisez

*PRESENT PARTICIPLE*
suffisant

*PRESENT*

| | |
|---|---|
| je | suffis |
| tu | suffis |
| il | suffit |
| nous | suffisons |
| vous | suffisez |
| ils | suffisent |

*IMPERFECT*

| | |
|---|---|
| je | suffisais |
| tu | suffisais |
| il | suffisait |
| nous | suffisions |
| vous | suffisiez |
| ils | suffisaient |

*FUTURE*

| | |
|---|---|
| je | suffirai |
| tu | suffiras |
| il | suffira |
| nous | suffirons |
| vous | suffirez |
| ils | suffiront |

*CONDITIONAL*

| | |
|---|---|
| je | suffirais |
| tu | suffirais |
| il | suffirait |
| nous | suffirions |
| vous | suffiriez |
| ils | suffiraient |

*PRESENT SUBJUNCTIVE*

| | |
|---|---|
| je | suffise |
| tu | suffises |
| il | suffise |
| nous | suffisions |
| vous | suffisiez |
| ils | suffisent |

*PAST HISTORIC*

| | |
|---|---|
| je | suffis |
| tu | suffis |
| il | suffit |
| nous | suffîmes |
| vous | suffîtes |
| ils | suffirent |

**suivre** *to follow*  Auxiliary: **avoir**

| PAST PARTICIPLE | IMPERATIVE |
|---|---|
| suivi | suis |
| | suivons |
| PRESENT PARTICIPLE | suivez |
| suivant | |

PRESENT

| | |
|---|---|
| je | suis |
| tu | suis |
| il | suit |
| nous | suivons |
| vous | suivez |
| ils | suivent |

IMPERFECT

| | |
|---|---|
| je | suivais |
| tu | suivais |
| il | suivait |
| nous | suivions |
| vous | suiviez |
| ils | suivaient |

FUTURE

| | |
|---|---|
| je | suivrai |
| tu | suivras |
| il | suivra |
| nous | suivrons |
| vous | suivrez |
| ils | suivront |

CONDITIONAL

| | |
|---|---|
| je | suivrais |
| tu | suivrais |
| il | suivrait |
| nous | suivrions |
| vous | suivriez |
| ils | suivraient |

PRESENT SUBJUNCTIVE

| | |
|---|---|
| je | suive |
| tu | suives |
| il | suive |
| nous | suivions |
| vous | suiviez |
| ils | suivent |

PAST HISTORIC

| | |
|---|---|
| je | suivis |
| tu | suivis |
| il | suivit |
| nous | suivîmes |
| vous | suivîtes |
| ils | suivirent |

**se taire** *to stop talking*     Auxiliary: **être**

---

PAST PARTICIPLE
  tu

PRESENT PARTICIPLE
  se taisant

IMPERATIVE
  tais-toi
  taisons-nous
  taisez-vous

---

PRESENT
| je | me tais |
| tu | te tais |
| il | se tait |
| nous | nous taisons |
| vous | vous taisez |
| ils | se taisent |

IMPERFECT
| je | me taisais |
| tu | te taisais |
| il | se taisait |
| nous | nous taisions |
| vous | vous taisiez |
| ils | se taisaient |

FUTURE
| je | me tairai |
| tu | te tairas |
| il | se taira |
| nous | nous tairons |
| vous | vous tairez |
| ils | se tairont |

CONDITIONAL
| je | me tairais |
| tu | te tairais |
| il | se tairait |
| nous | nous tairions |
| vous | vous tairiez |
| ils | se tairaient |

PRESENT SUBJUNCTIVE
| je | me taise |
| tu | te taises |
| il | se taise |
| nous | nous taisions |
| vous | vous taisiez |
| ils | se taisent |

PAST HISTORIC
| je | me tus |
| tu | te tus |
| il | se tut |
| nous | nous tûmes |
| vous | vous tûtes |
| ils | se turent |

**tenir** *to hold*  Auxiliary: **avoir**

---

*PAST PARTICIPLE*
tenu

*PRESENT PARTICIPLE*
tenant

*IMPERATIVE*
tiens
tenons
tenez

---

*PRESENT*

| | |
|---|---|
| je | tiens |
| tu | tiens |
| il | tient |
| nous | tenons |
| vous | tenez |
| ils | tiennent |

*FUTURE*

| | |
|---|---|
| je | tiendrai |
| tu | tiendras |
| il | tiendra |
| nous | tiendrons |
| vous | tiendrez |
| ils | tiendront |

*PRESENT SUBJUNCTIVE*

| | |
|---|---|
| je | tienne |
| tu | tiennes |
| il | tienne |
| nous | tenions |
| vous | teniez |
| ils | tiennent |

*IMPERFECT*

| | |
|---|---|
| je | tenais |
| tu | tenais |
| il | tenait |
| nous | tenions |
| vous | teniez |
| ils | tenaient |

*CONDITIONAL*

| | |
|---|---|
| je | tiendrais |
| tu | tiendrais |
| il | tiendrait |
| nous | tiendrions |
| vous | tiendriez |
| ils | tiendraient |

*PAST HISTORIC*

| | |
|---|---|
| je | tins |
| tu | tins |
| il | tint |
| nous | tînmes |
| vous | tîntes |
| ils | tinrent |

**vaincre** *to defeat*                    Auxiliary: **avoir**

---

*PAST PARTICIPLE*
vaincu

*PRESENT PARTICIPLE*
vainquant

*IMPERATIVE*
vaincs
vainquons
vainquez

---

*PRESENT*
|      |            |
|------|------------|
| je   | vaincs     |
| tu   | vaincs     |
| il   | vainc      |
| nous | vainquons  |
| vous | vainquez   |
| ils  | vainquent  |

*FUTURE*
|      |            |
|------|------------|
| je   | vaincrai   |
| tu   | vaincras   |
| il   | vaincra    |
| nous | vaincrons  |
| vous | vaincrez   |
| ils  | vaincront  |

*PRESENT SUBJUNCTIVE*
|      |            |
|------|------------|
| je   | vainque    |
| tu   | vainques   |
| il   | vainque    |
| nous | vainquions |
| vous | vainquiez  |
| ils  | vainquent  |

*IMPERFECT*
|      |             |
|------|-------------|
| je   | vainquais   |
| tu   | vainquais   |
| il   | vainquait   |
| nous | vainquions  |
| vous | vainquiez   |
| ils  | vainquaient |

*CONDITIONAL*
|      |             |
|------|-------------|
| je   | vaincrais   |
| tu   | vaincrais   |
| il   | vaincrait   |
| nous | vaincrions  |
| vous | vaincriez   |
| ils  | vaincraient |

*PAST HISTORIC*
|      |             |
|------|-------------|
| je   | vainquis    |
| tu   | vainquis    |
| il   | vainquit    |
| nous | vainquîmes  |
| vous | vainquîtes  |
| ils  | vainquirent |

## **valoir** *to be worth*      Auxiliary: **avoir**

*PAST PARTICIPLE*
valu

*PRESENT PARTICIPLE*
valant

*IMPERATIVE*
vaux
valons
valez

| *PRESENT* | | *IMPERFECT* | |
|---|---|---|---|
| je | vaux | je | valais |
| tu | vaux | tu | valais |
| il | vaut | il | valait |
| nous | valons | nous | valions |
| vous | valez | vous | valiez |
| ils | valent | ils | valaient |

| *FUTURE* | | *CONDITIONAL* | |
|---|---|---|---|
| je | vaudrai | je | vaudrais |
| tu | vaudras | tu | vaudrais |
| il | vaudra | il | vaudrait |
| nous | vaudrons | nous | vaudrions |
| vous | vaudrez | vous | vaudriez |
| ils | vaudront | ils | vaudraient |

| *PRESENT SUBJUNCTIVE* | | *PAST HISTORIC* | |
|---|---|---|---|
| je | vaille | je | valus |
| tu | vailles | tu | valus |
| il | vaille | il | valut |
| nous | valions | nous | valûmes |
| vous | valiez | vous | valûtes |
| ils | vaillent | ils | valurent |

**venir** *to come*                          Auxiliary: **être**

PAST PARTICIPLE
 **venu**

PRESENT PARTICIPLE
 **venant**

IMPERATIVE
 **viens**
 **venons**
 **venez**

PRESENT
|       |          |
|-------|----------|
| je    | viens    |
| tu    | viens    |
| il    | vient    |
| nous  | venons   |
| vous  | venez    |
| ils   | viennent |

IMPERFECT
|       |          |
|-------|----------|
| je    | venais   |
| tu    | venais   |
| il    | venait   |
| nous  | venions  |
| vous  | veniez   |
| ils   | venaient |

FUTURE
|       |           |
|-------|-----------|
| je    | viendrai  |
| tu    | viendras  |
| il    | viendra   |
| nous  | viendrons |
| vous  | viendrez  |
| ils   | viendront |

CONDITIONAL
|       |             |
|-------|-------------|
| je    | viendrais   |
| tu    | viendrais   |
| il    | viendrait   |
| nous  | viendrions  |
| vous  | viendriez   |
| ils   | viendraient |

PRESENT SUBJUNCTIVE
|       |          |
|-------|----------|
| je    | vienne   |
| tu    | viennes  |
| il    | vienne   |
| nous  | venions  |
| vous  | veniez   |
| ils   | viennent |

PAST HISTORIC
|       |         |
|-------|---------|
| je    | vins    |
| tu    | vins    |
| il    | vint    |
| nous  | vînmes  |
| vous  | vîntes  |
| ils   | vinrent |

## vêtir *to dress* Auxiliary: avoir

PAST PARTICIPLE
vêtu

PRESENT PARTICIPLE
vêtant

IMPERATIVE
vêts
vêtons
vêtez

| PRESENT | | IMPERFECT | |
|---|---|---|---|
| je | vêts | je | vêtais |
| tu | vêts | tu | vêtais |
| il | vêt | il | vêtait |
| nous | vêtons | nous | vêtions |
| vous | vêtez | vous | vêtiez |
| ils | vêtent | ils | vêtaient |

| FUTURE | | CONDITIONAL | |
|---|---|---|---|
| je | vêtirai | je | vêtirais |
| tu | vêtiras | tu | vêtirais |
| il | vêtira | il | vêtirait |
| nous | vêtirons | nous | vêtirions |
| vous | vêtirez | vous | vêtiriez |
| ils | vêtiront | ils | vêtiraient |

| PRESENT SUBJUNCTIVE | | PAST HISTORIC | |
|---|---|---|---|
| je | vête | je | vêtis |
| tu | vêtes | tu | vêtis |
| il | vête | il | vêtit |
| nous | vêtions | nous | vêtîmes |
| vous | vêtiez | vous | vêtîtes |
| ils | vêtent | ils | vêtirent |

**vivre** *to live*                         Auxiliary: **avoir**

---

PAST PARTICIPLE
**vécu**

PRESENT PARTICIPLE
**vivant**

IMPERATIVE
**vis**
vivons
vivez

---

| PRESENT | | IMPERFECT | |
|---|---|---|---|
| je | **vis** | je | vivais |
| tu | **vis** | tu | vivais |
| il | **vit** | il | vivait |
| nous | vivons | nous | vivions |
| vous | vivez | vous | viviez |
| ils | vivent | ils | vivaient |

| FUTURE | | CONDITIONAL | |
|---|---|---|---|
| je | vivrai | je | vivrais |
| tu | vivras | tu | vivrais |
| il | vivra | il | vivrait |
| nous | vivrons | nous | vivrions |
| vous | vivrez | vous | vivriez |
| ils | vivront | ils | vivraient |

| PRESENT SUBJUNCTIVE | | PAST HISTORIC | |
|---|---|---|---|
| je | vive | je | **vécus** |
| tu | vives | tu | **vécus** |
| il | vive | il | **vécut** |
| nous | vivions | nous | **vécûmes** |
| vous | viviez | vous | **vécûtes** |
| ils | vivent | ils | **vécurent** |

**voir** *to see*        Auxiliary: **avoir**

---

*PAST PARTICIPLE*
**vu**

*PRESENT PARTICIPLE*
**voyant**

*IMPERATIVE*
**vois**
**voyons**
**voyez**

---

*PRESENT*

| | |
|---|---|
| je | vois |
| tu | vois |
| il | voit |
| nous | voyons |
| vous | voyez |
| ils | voient |

*FUTURE*

| | |
|---|---|
| je | verrai |
| tu | verras |
| il | verra |
| nous | verrons |
| vous | verrez |
| ils | verront |

*PRESENT SUBJUNCTIVE*

| | |
|---|---|
| je | voie |
| tu | voies |
| il | voie |
| nous | voyions |
| vous | voyiez |
| ils | voient |

*IMPERFECT*

| | |
|---|---|
| je | voyais |
| tu | voyais |
| il | voyait |
| nous | voyions |
| vous | voyiez |
| ils | voyaient |

*CONDITIONAL*

| | |
|---|---|
| je | verrais |
| tu | verrais |
| il | verrait |
| nous | verrions |
| vous | verriez |
| ils | verraient |

*PAST HISTORIC*

| | |
|---|---|
| je | vis |
| tu | vis |
| il | vit |
| nous | vîmes |
| vous | vîtes |
| ils | virent |

**vouloir** *to wish, want*      Auxiliary: **avoir**

*PAST PARTICIPLE*
voulu

*IMPERATIVE*
  veuille
  veuillons
  veuillez

*PRESENT PARTICIPLE*
voulant

*PRESENT*

| | |
|---|---|
| je | veux |
| tu | veux |
| il | veut |
| nous | voulons |
| vous | voulez |
| ils | veulent |

*IMPERFECT*

| | |
|---|---|
| je | voulais |
| tu | voulais |
| il | voulait |
| nous | voulions |
| vous | vouliez |
| ils | voulaient |

*FUTURE*

| | |
|---|---|
| je | voudrai |
| tu | voudras |
| il | voudra |
| nous | voudrons |
| vous | voudrez |
| ils | voudront |

*CONDITIONAL*

| | |
|---|---|
| je | voudrais |
| tu | voudrais |
| il | voudrait |
| nous | voudrions |
| vous | voudriez |
| ils | voudraient |

*PRESENT SUBJUNCTIVE*

| | |
|---|---|
| je | veuille |
| tu | veuilles |
| il | veuille |
| nous | voulions |
| vous | vouliez |
| ils | veuillent |

*PAST HISTORIC*

| | |
|---|---|
| je | voulus |
| tu | voulus |
| il | voulut |
| nous | voulûmes |
| vous | voulûtes |
| ils | voulurent |

## The Gender of Nouns

In French, all nouns are either masculine or feminine, whether
denoting people, animals or things. Unlike English, there is no neuter
gender for inanimate objects and abstract nouns.

Gender is largely unpredictable and has to be learnt for each noun.
However, the following guidelines will help you determine the gender
for certain types of nouns.

● Nouns denoting male people and animals are usually – but not
  always – masculine, e.g.

  **un homme**          **un taureau**
  *a man*               *a bull*
  **un infirmier**      **un cheval**
  *a (male) nurse*      *a horse*

● Nouns denoting female people and animals are usually – but not
  always – feminine, e.g.

  **une fille**         **une vache**
  *a girl*              *a cow*
  **une infirmière**    **une brebis**
  *a nurse*             *a ewe*

● Some nouns are masculine OR feminine depending on the sex of
  the person to whom they refer, e.g.

  **un camarade**       **une camarade**
  *a (male) friend*     *a (female) friend*
  **un Belge**          **une Belge**
  *a Belgian (man)*     *a Belgian (woman)*

● Other nouns referring to either men or women have only one
  gender which applies to both, e.g.

  **un professeur**     **une personne**      **une sentinelle**
  *a teacher*           *a person*            *a sentry*
  **un témoin**         **une victime**       **une recrue**
  *a witness*           *a victim*            *a recruit*

● Sometimes the ending of the noun indicates its gender. Shown below are some of the most important to guide you:

**Masculine endings**

| | |
|---|---|
| -age | **le courage** *courage*, **le rinçage** *rinsing* |
| | *EXCEPTIONS:* **une cage** *a cage*, **une image** *a picture*, **la nage** *swimming*, **une page** *a page*, **une plage** *a beach*, **une rage** *a rage* |
| -ment | **le commencement** *the beginning* |
| | *EXCEPTION:* **une jument** *a mare* |
| -oir | **un couloir** *a corridor*, **un miroir** *a mirror* |
| -sme | **le pessimisme** *pessimism*, **l'enthousiasme** *enthusiasm* |

**Feminine endings**

| | |
|---|---|
| -ance, anse | **la confiance** *confidence*, **la danse** *dancing* |
| -ence, -ense | **la prudence** *caution*, **la défense** *defence* |
| | *EXCEPTION:* **le silence** *silence* |
| -ion | **une région** *a region*, **une addition** *a bill* |
| | *EXCEPTIONS:* **un pion** *a pawn*, **un espion** *a spy* |
| -oire | **une baignoire** *a bath(tub)* |
| -té, -tié | **la beauté** *beauty*, **la moitié** *half* |

● Suffixes which differentiate between male and female are shown on pp. 134 and 136

● The following words have different meanings depending on gender:

| | | | |
|---|---|---|---|
| **le crêpe** | *crêpe* | **la crêpe** | *pancake* |
| **le livre** | *book* | **la livre** | *pound* |
| **le manche** | *handle* | **la manche** | *sleeve* |
| **le mode** | *method* | **la mode** | *fashion* |
| **le moule** | *mould* | **la moule** | *mussel* |
| **le page** | *page(boy)* | **la page** | *page* (in book) |
| **le physique** | *physique* | **la physique** | *physics* |
| **le poêle** | *stove* | **la poêle** | *frying pan* |
| **le somme** | *nap* | **la somme** | *sum* |
| **le tour** | *turn* | **la tour** | *tower* |
| **le voile** | *veil* | **la voile** | *sail* |

# Gender: the formation of feminines

As in English, male and female are sometimes differentiated by the use of two quite separate words, e.g.

| | |
|---|---|
| **mon oncle** | **ma tante** |
| *my uncle* | *my aunt* |
| **un taureau** | **une vache** |
| *a bull* | *a cow* |

There are, however, some words in French which show this distinction by the form of their ending

● Some nouns add an **e** to the masculine singular form to form the feminine (→ **1**)

● If the masculine singular form already ends in **-e**, no further **e** is added in the feminine (→ **2**)

● Some nouns undergo a further change when **e** is added. These changes occur regularly and are shown on p. 136

**Feminine forms to note**

| MASCULINE | FEMININE | |
|---|---|---|
| **un âne** | **une ânesse** | *donkey* |
| **le comte** | **la comtesse** | *count/countess* |
| **le duc** | **la duchesse** | *duke/duchess* |
| **un Esquimau** | **une Esquimaude** | *Eskimo* |
| **le fou** | **la folle** | *madman/madwoman* |
| **le Grec** | **la Grecque** | *Greek* |
| **un hôte** | **une hôtesse** | *host/hostess* |
| **le jumeau** | **la jumelle** | *twin* |
| **le maître** | **la maîtresse** | *master/mistress* |
| **le prince** | **la princesse** | *prince/princess* |
| **le tigre** | **la tigresse** | *tiger/tigress* |
| **le traître** | **la traîtresse** | *traitor* |
| **le Turc** | **la Turque** | *Turk* |
| **le vieux** | **la vieille** | *old man/old woman* |

*Continued*

**1 un ami**
a (male) friend
**un employé**
a (male) employee
**un Français**
a Frenchman

**une amie**
a (female) friend
**une employée**
a (female) employee
**une Française**
a Frenchwoman

**2 un élève**
a (male) pupil
**un collègue**
a (male) colleague
**un camarade**
a (male) friend

**une élève**
a (female) pupil
**une collègue**
a (female) colleague
**une camarade**
a (female) friend

## Regular feminine endings

| MASC. SING. | FEM. SING. | |
|---|---|---|
| -f | -ve | (→ 1) |
| -x | -se | (→ 2) |
| -eur | -euse | (→ 3) |
| -teur | ⎰ -teuse | (→ 4) |
|  | ⎱ -trice | (→ 5) |

Some nouns double the final consonant before adding **e**:

| MASC. SING. | FEM. SING. | |
|---|---|---|
| -an | -anne | (→ 6) |
| -en | -enne | (→ 7) |
| -on | -onne | (→ 8) |
| -et | -ette | (→ 9) |
| -el | -elle | (→ 10) |

Some nouns add an accent to the final syllable before adding **e**:

| MASC. SING. | FEM. SING. | |
|---|---|---|
| -er | -ère | (→ 11) |

### Pronunciation and feminine endings

This is dealt with on p. 244.

1 **un sportif**
a sportsman
**un veuf**
a widower

**une sportive**
a sportswoman
**une veuve**
a widow

2 **un époux**
a husband
**un amoureux**
a man in love

**une épouse**
a wife
**une amoureuse**
a woman in love

3 **un danseur**
a dancer
**un voleur**
a thief

**une danseuse**
a dancer
**une voleuse**
a thief

4 **un menteur**
a liar
**un chanteur**
a singer

**une menteuse**
a liar
**une chanteuse**
a singer

5 **un acteur**
an actor
**un conducteur**
a driver

**une actrice**
an actress
**une conductrice**
a driver

6 **un paysan**
a countryman

**une paysanne**
a countrywoman

7 **un Parisien**
a Parisian

**une Parisienne**
a Parisian (woman)

8 **un baron**
a baron

**une baronne**
a baroness

9 **le cadet**
the youngest (child)

**la cadette**
the youngest (child)

10 **un intellectuel**
an intellectual

**une intellectuelle**
an intellectual

11 **un étranger**
a foreigner
**le dernier**
the last (one)

**une étrangère**
a foreigner
**la dernière**
the last (one)

## The formation of plurals

● Most nouns add **s** to the singular form (→ **1**)

● When the singular form already ends in **-s**, **-x** or **-z**, no further **s** is added (→ **2**)

● For nouns ending in **-au**, **-eau** or **-eu**, the plural ends in **-aux**, **-eaux** or **-eux** (→ **3**)
  Exceptions:  **pneu**      *tyre*      (plur: **pneus**)
               **bleu**      *bruise*    (plur: **bleus**)

● For nouns ending in **-al** or **-ail**, the plural ends in **-aux** (→ **4**)
  Exceptions:  **bal**        *ball*      (plur: **bals**)
               **festival**   *festival*  (plur: **festivals**)
               **chandail**   *sweater*   (plur: **chandails**)
               **détail**     *detail*    (plur: **détails**)

● Forming the plural of compound nouns is complicated and you are advised to check each one individually in a dictionary

### Irregular plural forms

● Some masculine nouns ending in **-ou** add **x** in the plural. These are:
  **bijou**   *jewel*    **genou**   *knee*    **joujou**   *toy*
  **caillou** *pebble*   **hibou**   *owl*     **pou**      *louse*
  **chou**    *cabbage*

● Some other nouns are totally unpredictable. Chief among these are:

| SINGULAR | PLURAL |
|---|---|
| **œil** *eye* | **yeux** |
| **ciel** *sky* | **cieux** |
| **Monsieur** *Mr.* | **Messieurs** |
| **Madame** *Mrs.* | **Mesdames** |
| **Mademoiselle** *Miss* | **Mesdemoiselles** |

### Pronunciation of plural forms
This is dealt with on p. 244

1 **le jardin**
the garden
**une voiture**
a car
**l'hôtel**
the hotel

**les jardins**
the gardens
**des voitures**
(some) cars
**les hôtels**
the hotels

2 **un tas**
a heap
**une voix**
a voice
**le gaz**
the gas

**des tas**
(some) heaps
**des voix**
(some) voices
**les gaz**
the gases

3 **un tuyau**
a pipe
**le chapeau**
the hat
**le feu**
the fire

**des tuyaux**
(some) pipes
**les chapeaux**
the hats
**les feux**
the fires

4 **le journal**
the newspaper
**un travail**
a job

**les journaux**
the newspapers
**des travaux**
(some) jobs

## The Definite Article

|        | WITH<br>MASC. NOUN | WITH<br>FEM. NOUN |       |
|--------|------------|-----------|-------|
| SING.  | le (l')    | la (l')   | the   |
| PLUR.  | les        | les       | the   |

● The gender and number of the noun determines the form of the article (→ **1**)

● **le** and **la** change to **l'** before a vowel or an **h** 'mute' (→ **2**)

● For uses of the definite article see p. 142

● à + le/la (l'), à + les

|        | WITH<br>MASC. NOUN | WITH<br>FEM. NOUN |        |
|--------|------------|-----------|--------|
| SING.  | au (à l')  | à la (à l')|        |
| PLUR.  | aux        | aux       | (→ **3**) |

● The definite article combines with the preposition **à**, as shown above. You should pay particular attention to the masculine singular form **au**, and both plural forms **aux**, since these are not visually the sum of their parts

● de + le/la (l'), de + les

|        | WITH<br>MASC. NOUN | WITH<br>FEM. NOUN |        |
|--------|------------|-----------|--------|
| SING.  | du (de l') | de la (de l')|      |
| PLUR.  | des        | des       | (→ **4**) |

● The definite article combines with the preposition **de**, as shown above. You should pay particular attention to the masculine singular form **du**, and both plural forms **des**, since these are not visually the sum of their parts

*Continued*

| MASCULINE | FEMININE |
|---|---|
| **1 le train** | **la gare** |
| the train | the station |
| **le garçon** | **la fille** |
| the boy | the girl |
| **les hôtels** | **les écoles** |
| the hotels | the schools |
| **les professeurs** | **les femmes** |
| the teachers | the women |
| **2 l'acteur** | **l'actrice** |
| the actor | the actress |
| **l'effet** | **l'eau** |
| the effect | the water |
| **l'ingrédient** | **l'idée** |
| the ingredient | the idea |
| **l'objet** | **l'ombre** |
| the object | the shadow |
| **l'univers** | **l'usine** |
| the universe | the factory |
| **l'hôpital** | **l'heure** |
| the hospital | the time |
| **3 au cinéma** | **à la bibliothèque** |
| at/to the cinema | at/to the library |
| **à l'employé** | **à l'infirmière** |
| to the employee | to the nurse |
| **à l'hôpital** | **à l'hôtesse** |
| at/to the hospital | to the hostess |
| **aux étudiants** | **aux maisons** |
| to the students | to the houses |
| **4 du bureau** | **de la réunion** |
| from/of the office | from/of the meeting |
| **de l'auteur** | **de l'Italienne** |
| from/of the author | from/of the Italian woman |
| **de l'hôte** | **de l'horloge** |
| from/of the host | of the clock |
| **des Etats-Unis** | **des vendeuses** |
| from/of the United States | from/of the saleswomen |

## Uses of the definite article

While the definite article is used in much the same way in French as it is in English, its use is more widespread in French. Unlike English the definite article is also used:

- with abstract nouns, except when following certain prepositions (→ 1)

- in generalisations, especially with plural or uncountable* nouns (→ 2)

- with names of countries (→ 3)
  Exceptions: no article with countries following **en** *to/in* (→ 4)

- with parts of the body (→ 5)
  'Ownership' is often indicated by an indirect object pronoun or a reflexive pronoun (→ 6)

- in expressions of quantity/rate/price (→ 7)

- with titles/ranks/professions followed by a proper name (→ 8)

- The definite article is NOT used with nouns in apposition (→ 9)

*An uncountable noun is one which cannot be used in the plural or with an indefinite article, e.g. **l'acier** *steel*, **le lait** *milk*

1 **Les prix montent**
Prices are rising
**L'amour rayonne dans ses yeux**
Love shines in his eyes
*BUT*  **avec plaisir**  **sans espoir**
with pleasure  without hope

2 **Je n'aime pas le café**
I don't like coffee
**Les enfants ont besoin d'être aimés**
Children need to be loved

3 **le Japon**  **la France**  **l'Italie**  **les Pays-Bas**
Japan  France  Italy  The Netherlands

4 **aller en Ecosse**  **Il travaille en Allemagne**
to go to Scotland  He works in Germany

5 **Tournez la tête à gauche**
Turn your head to the left
**J'ai mal à la gorge**
My throat is sore, I have a sore throat

6 **La tête me tourne**
My head is spinning
**Elle s'est brossé les dents**
She brushed her teeth

7 **40 francs le mètre / le kilo / la douzaine / la pièce**
40 francs a metre / a kilo / a dozen / each
**rouler à 80 km à l'heure**
to go at 50 m.p.h.
**payé à l'heure / au jour / au mois**
paid by the hour / by the day / by the month

8 **le roi Georges III**  **le capitaine Darbeau**
King George III  Captain Darbeau
**le docteur Rousseau**  **Monsieur le président**
Dr. Rousseau  Mr. Chairman / President

9 **Victor Hugo, grand écrivain du dix-neuvième siècle**
Victor Hugo, a great author of the nineteenth century
**Joseph Leblanc, inventeur et entrepreneur, a été le premier ...**
Joseph Leblanc, an inventor and entrepreneur, was the first ...

# The Partitive Article

The partitive article has the sense of *some* or *any*, although the French is not always translated in English.

**Forms of the partitive**

|  | WITH MASC. NOUN | WITH FEM. NOUN |  |
|---|---|---|---|
| SING. | du (de l') | de la (de l') | some, any |
| PLUR. | des | des | some, any |

● The gender and number of the noun determines the form of the partitive (→ **1**)

● The forms shown in brackets are used before a vowel or an **h** 'mute' (→ **2**)

● **des** becomes **de** (**d'** + vowel) before an adjective (→ **3**), unless the adjective and noun are seen as forming one unit (→ **4**)

● In negative sentences **de** (**d'** + vowel) is used for both genders, singular and plural (→ **5**)
  Exception: after **ne ... que** *only*, the positive forms above are used (→ **6**)

1 **Avez-vous du sucre?**
 Have you any sugar?
 **J'ai acheté de la farine et de la margarine**
 I bought (some) flour and margarine
 **Il a mangé des gâteaux**
 He ate some cakes
 **Est-ce qu'il y a des lettres pour moi?**
 Are there (any) letters for me?

2 **Il me doit de l'argent**      **C'est de l'histoire ancienne**
 He owes me (some) money      That's ancient history

3 **Il a fait de gros efforts pour nous aider**
 He made a great effort to help us
 **Cette région a de belles églises**
 This region has some beautiful churches

4 **des grandes vacances**      **des jeunes gens**
 summer holidays      young people

5 **Je n'ai pas de nourriture/d'argent**
 I don't have any food/money
 **Vous n'avez pas de timbres/d'œufs?**
 Have you no stamps/eggs?
 **Je ne mange jamais de viande/d'omelettes**
 I never eat meat/omelettes
 **Il ne veut plus de visiteurs/d'eau**
 He doesn't want any more visitors/water

6 **Il ne boit que du thé/de la bière/de l'eau**
 He only drinks tea/beer/water
 **Je n'ai que des problèmes avec cette machine**
 I have nothing but problems with this machine

# ARTICLES

## The Indefinite Article

|  | WITH MASC. NOUN | WITH FEM. NOUN |  |
|---|---|---|---|
| SING. | un | une | a |
| PLUR. | des | des | some |

● **des** is also the plural of the partitive article (see p. 144)

● In negative sentences, **de** (**d'** + vowel) is used for both singular and plural (→ **1**)

● The indefinite article is used in French largely as it is in English EXCEPT:

– there is no article when a person's profession is being stated (→ **2**)
  The article *is* present however, following **ce** (**c'** + vowel) (→ **3**)

– the English article is not translated by **un/une** in constructions like *what a surprise*, *what an idiot* (→ **4**)

– in structures of the type given in example **5** the article **un/une** is used in French and not translated in English (→ **5**)

1  **Je n'ai pas de livre/d'enfants**
   I don't have a book/(any) children

2  **Il est professeur**                    **Ma mère est infirmière**
   He's a teacher                           My mother's a nurse

3  **C'est un médecin**
   He's/She's a doctor
   **Ce sont des acteurs**
   They're actors

4  **Quelle surprise!**                     **Quel dommage!**
   What a surprise!                         What a shame!

5  **avec une grande sagesse/un courage admirable**
   with great wisdom/admirable courage
   **Il a fait preuve d'un sang-froid incroyable**
   He showed incredible coolness
   **Un produit d'une qualité incomparable**
   A product of incomparable quality

# Adjectives

Most adjectives agree in number and in gender with the noun or pronoun.

### The formation of feminines

● Most adjectives add an **e** to the masculine singular form (→ **1**)

● If the masculine singular form already ends in **-e**, no further **e** is added (→ **2**)

● Some adjectives undergo a further change when **e** is added. These changes occur regularly and are shown on p. 150

● Irregular feminine forms are shown on p. 152

### The formation of plurals

● The plural of both regular and irregular adjectives is formed by adding an **s** to the masculine or feminine singular form, as appropriate (→ **3**)

● When the masculine singular form already ends in **-s** or **-x**, no further **s** is added (→ **4**)

● For masculine singulars ending in **-au** and **-eau**, the masculine plural is **-aux** and **-eaux** (→ **5**)

● For masculine singulars ending in **-al**, the masculine plural is **-aux** (→ **6**)

    Exceptions:  **final**   (masculine plural **finals**)
                 **fatal**   (masculine plural **fatals**)
                 **naval**   (masculine plural **navals**)

### Pronunciation of feminine and plural adjectives
This is dealt with on p. 244

1 **mon frère aîné**
my elder brother
**le petit garçon**
the little boy
**un sac gris**
a grey bag
**un bruit fort**
a loud noise

   **ma sœur aînée**
my elder sister
**la petite fille**
the little girl
**une chemise grise**
a grey shirt
**une voix forte**
a loud voice

2 **un jeune homme**
a young man
**l'autre verre**
the other glass

   **une jeune femme**
a young woman
**l'autre assiette**
the other plate

3 **le dernier train**
the last train
**une vieille maison**
an old house
**un long voyage**
a long journey
**la rue étroite**
the narrow street

   **les derniers trains**
the last trains
**de vieilles maisons**
old houses
**de longs voyages**
long journeys
**les rues étroites**
the narrow streets

4 **un diplomate français**
a French diplomat
**un homme dangereux**
a dangerous man

   **des diplomates français**
French diplomats
**des hommes dangereux**
dangerous men

5 **le nouveau professeur**
the new teacher
**un chien esquimau**
a husky (Fr. = an Eskimo dog)

   **les nouveaux professeurs**
the new teachers
**des chiens esquimaux**
huskies (Fr. = Eskimo dogs)

6 **un ami loyal**
a loyal friend
**un geste amical**
a friendly gesture

   **des amis loyaux**
loyal friends
**des gestes amicaux**
friendly gestures

## Regular feminine endings

| MASC. SING. | FEM. SING. | EXAMPLES | |
|---|---|---|---|
| -f | -ve | **neuf, vif** | (→ 1) |
| -x | -se | **heureux, jaloux** | (→ 2) |
| -eur | -euse | **travailleur, flâneur** | (→ 3) |
| -teur | ⌠ -teuse | **flatteur, menteur** | (→ 4) |
| | ⌡ -trice | **destructeur, séducteur** | (→ 5) |

Exceptions:

**bref**: see p. 152

**doux**, **faux**, **roux**, **vieux**: see p. 152

**extérieur**, **inférieur**, **intérieur**, **meilleur**, **supérieur**: all add **e** to the masculine

**enchanteur**: fem. = **enchanteresse**

| MASC. SING. | FEM. SING. | EXAMPLES | |
|---|---|---|---|
| -an | -anne | **paysan** | (→ 6) |
| -en | -enne | **ancien, parisien** | (→ 7) |
| -on | -onne | **bon, breton** | (→ 8) |
| -as | -asse | **bas, las** | (→ 9) |
| -et* | -ette | **muet, violet** | (→ 10) |
| -el | -elle | **annuel, mortel** | (→ 11) |
| -eil | -eille | **pareil, vermeil** | (→ 12) |

Exception:

**ras**: fem. = **rase**

| MASC. SING. | FEM. SING. | EXAMPLES | |
|---|---|---|---|
| -et* | -ète | **secret, complet** | (→ 13) |
| -er | -ère | **étranger, fier** | (→ 14) |

*Note that there are two feminine endings for masculine adjectives ending in **-et**.

1 **un résultat positif**
a positive result

**une attitude positive**
a positive attitude

2 **d'un ton sérieux**
in a serious tone (of voice)

**une voix sérieuse**
a serious voice

3 **un enfant trompeur**
a deceitful child

**une déclaration trompeuse**
a misleading statement

4 **un tableau flatteur**
a flattering picture

**une comparaison flatteuse**
a flattering comparison

5 **un geste protecteur**
a protective gesture

**une couche protectrice**
a protective layer

6 **un problème paysan**
a farming problem

**la vie paysanne**
country life

7 **un avion égyptien**
an Egyptian plane

**une statue égyptienne**
an Egyptian statue

8 **un bon repas**
a good meal

**de bonne humeur**
in a good mood

9 **un plafond bas**
a low ceiling

**à voix basse**
in a low voice

10 **un travail net**
a clean piece of work

**une explication nette**
a clear explanation

11 **un homme cruel**
a cruel man

**une remarque cruelle**
a cruel remark

12 **un livre pareil**
such a book

**en pareille occasion**
on such an occasion

13 **un regard inquiet**
an anxious look

**une attente inquiète**
an anxious wait

14 **un goût amer**
a bitter taste

**une amère déception**
a bitter disappointment

## Adjectives with irregular feminine forms

| MASC. SING. | FEM. SING. | | |
|---|---|---|---|
| aigu | aiguë | sharp; high-pitched | (→ 1) |
| ambigu | ambiguë | ambiguous | |
| beau (bel)* | belle | beautiful | |
| bénin | bénigne | benign | |
| blanc | blanche | white | |
| bref | brève | brief, short | (→ 2) |
| doux | douce | soft; sweet | |
| épais | épaisse | think | |
| esquimau | esquimaude | Eskimo | |
| faux | fausse | wrong | |
| favori | favorite | favourite | (→ 3) |
| fou (fol)* | folle | mad | |
| frais | fraîche | fresh | (→ 4) |
| franc | franche | frank | |
| gentil | gentille | kind | |
| grec | grecque | Greek | |
| gros | grosse | big | |
| jumeau | jumelle | twin | (→ 5) |
| long | longue | long | |
| malin | maligne | malignant | |
| mou (mol)* | molle | soft | |
| nouveau (nouvel)* | nouvelle | new | |
| nul | nulle | no | |
| public | publique | public | (→ 6) |
| roux | rousse | red-haired | |
| sec | sèche | dry | |
| sot | sotte | foolish | |
| turc | turque | Turkish | |
| vieux (vieil)* | vieille | old | |

*This form is used when the following word begins with a vowel or an **h** 'mute' (→ 7)

1 **un son aigu**
a high-pitched sound

**une douleur aiguë**
a sharp pain

2 **un bref discours**
a short speech

**une brève rencontre**
a short meeting

3 **mon sport favori**
my favourite sport

**ma chanson favorite**
my favourite song

4 **du pain frais**
fresh bread

**de la crème fraîche**
fresh cream

5 **mon frère jumeau**
my twin brother

**ma sœur jumelle**
my twin sister

6 **un jardin public**
a (public) park

**l'opinion publique**
public opinion

7 **un bel appartement**
a beautiful flat
**le nouvel inspecteur**
the new inspector
**un vieil arbre**
an old tree

**un bel habit**
a beautiful outfit
**un nouvel harmonica**
a new harmonica
**un vieil hôtel**
an old hotel

## Comparatives and Superlatives

**Comparatives**
These are formed using the following constructions:

| | | |
|---|---|---|
| **plus ... (que)** | *more ... (than)* | (→ 1) |
| **moins ... (que)** | *less ... (than)* | (→ 2) |
| **aussi ... que** | *as ... as* | (→ 3) |
| **si ... que\*** | *as ... as* | (→ 4) |

\*used mainly after a negative

**Superlatives**
These are formed using the following constructions:

| | | |
|---|---|---|
| **le/la/les plus ... (que)** | *the most ... (that)* | (→ 5) |
| **le/la/les moins ... (que)** | *the least ... (that)* | (→ 6) |

- When the possessive adjective is present, two constructions are possible (→ 7)
- After a superlative the preposition **de** is often translated as *in* (→ 8)
- If a clause follows a superlative, the verb is in the subjunctive (→ 9)

**Adjectives with irregular comparatives / superlatives**

| ADJECTIVE | COMPARATIVE | SUPERLATIVE |
|---|---|---|
| **bon** | **meilleur** | **le meilleur** |
| *good* | *better* | *the best* |
| **mauvais** | **pire** OR | **le pire** OR |
| *bad* | **plus mauvais** | **le plus mauvais** |
| | *worse* | *the worst* |
| **petit** | **moindre\*** OR | **le moindre\*** OR |
| *small* | **plus petit** | **le plus petit** |
| | *smaller;* | *the smallest;* |
| | *lesser* | *the least* |

\*used only with abstract nouns

- Comparative and superlative adjectives agree in number and in gender with the noun, just like any other adjective (→ 10)

1 **une raison plus grave**
a more serious reason
**Elle est plus petite que moi**
She is smaller than me

2 **un film moins connu**
a less well-known film
**C'est moins cher qu'il ne pense**
It's cheaper than he thinks

3 **Robert était aussi inquiet que moi**
Robert was as worried as I was
**Cette ville n'est pas aussi grande que Bordeaux**
This town isn't as big as Bordeaux

4 **Ils ne sont pas si contents que ça**
They aren't as happy as all that

5 **le guide le plus utile**                    **la voiture la plus petite**
the most useful guidebook                the smallest car
**les plus grandes maisons**
the biggest houses

6 **le mois le moins agréable**                 **la fille la moins forte**
the least pleasant month                 the weakest girl
**les moins belles peintures**
the least attractive paintings

7 **Mon désir le plus cher**  ⎫
   **Mon plus cher désir**     ⎬  **est de voyager**
                              ⎭
My dearest wish is to travel

8 **la plus grande gare de Londres**
the biggest station in London
**l'habitant le plus âgé du village / de la région**
the oldest inhabitant in the village / in the area

9 **la personne la plus gentille que je connaisse**
the nicest person I know

10 **les moindres difficultés**
the least difficulties
**la meilleure qualité**
the best quality

## Demonstrative Adjectives

|  | MASCULINE | FEMININE |  |
|---|---|---|---|
| SING. | ce (cet) | cette | *this; that* |
| PLUR. | ces | ces | *these; those* |

● Demonstrative adjectives agree in number and gender with the noun (→ 1)

● **cet** is used when the following word begins with a vowel or an **h** 'mute' (→ 2)

● For emphasis or in order to distinguish between people or objects, **-ci** or **-là** is added to the noun: **-ci** indicates proximity (usually translated *this*) and **là** distance (*that*) (→ 3)

1 **Ce stylo ne marche pas**
This/That pen isn't working
**Comment s'appelle cette entreprise?**
What's this/that company called?
**Ces livres sont les miens**
These/Those books are mine
**Ces couleurs sont plus jolies**
These/Those colours are nicer

2 **cet oiseau**
this/that bird
**cet article**
this/that article
**cet homme**
this/that man

3 **Combien coûte ce manteau-ci?**
How much is this coat?
**Je voudrais cinq de ces pommes-là**
I'd like five of those apples
**Est-ce que tu reconnais cette personne-là?**
Do you recognize that person?
**Mettez ces vêtements-ci dans cette valise-là**
Put these clothes in that case
**Ce garçon-là appartient à ce groupe-ci**
That boy belongs to this group

## Interrogative Adjectives

|  | MASCULINE | FEMININE |  |
|---|---|---|---|
| SING. | quel? | quelle? | what?; which? |
| PLUR. | quels? | quelles? | what?; which? |

● Interrogative adjectives agree in number and gender with the noun (→ 1)

● The forms shown above are also used in indirect questions (→ 2)

## Exclamatory Adjectives

|  | MASCULINE | FEMININE |  |
|---|---|---|---|
| SING. | quel! | quelle! | what (a)! |
| PLUR. | quels! | quelles! | what! |

● Exclamatory adjectives agree in number and gender with the noun (→ 3)

● For other exclamations, see p. 214

1 **Quel genre d'homme est-ce?**
  What type of man is he?
  **Quelle est leur décision?**
  What is their decision?
  **Vous jouez de quels instruments?**
  What instruments do you play?
  **Quelles offres avez-vous reçues?**
  What offers have you received?
  **Quel vin recommandez-vous?**
  Which wine do you recommend?
  **Quelles couleurs préférez-vous?**
  Which colours do you prefer?

2 **Je ne sais pas à quelle heure il est arrivé**
  I don't know what time he arrived
  **Dites-moi quels sont les livres les plus intéressants**
  Tell me which books are the most interesting

3 **Quel dommage!**
  What a pity!
  **Quelle idée!**
  What an idea!
  **Quels beaux livres vous avez!**
  What fine books you have!
  **Quelles jolies fleurs!**
  What nice flowers!

## Possessive Adjectives

| WITH SING. NOUN | | WITH PLUR. NOUN | |
| MASC. | FEM. | MASC./FEM. | |
| **mon** | **ma (mon)** | **mes** | *my* |
| **ton** | **ta (ton)** | **tes** | *your* |
| **son** | **sa (son)** | **ses** | *his; her; its* |
| **notre** | **notre** | **nos** | *our* |
| **votre** | **votre** | **vos** | *your* |
| **leur** | **leur** | **leurs** | *their* |

● Possessive adjectives agree in number and gender with the noun, NOT WITH THE OWNER (→ **1**)

● The forms shown in brackets are used when the following word begins with a vowel or an **h** 'mute' (→ **2**)

● **son**, **sa**, **ses** have the additional meaning of *one's* (→ **3**)

1 **Catherine a oublié son parapluie**
  Catherine has left her umbrella
  **Paul cherche sa montre**
  Paul's looking for his watch
  **Mon frère et ma sœur habitent à Glasgow**
  My brother and sister live in Glasgow
  **Est-ce que tes voisins ont vendu leur voiture?**
  Did your neighbours sell their car?
  **Rangez vos affaires**
  Put your things away

2 **mon appareil-photo**
  my camera
  **ton histoire**
  your story
  **son erreur**
  his/her mistake
  **mon autre sœur**
  my other sister

3 **perdre son équilibre**
  to lose one's balance
  **présenter ses excuses**
  to offer one's apologies

## Position of Adjectives

● French adjectives usually follow the noun (→ **1**)

● Adjectives of colour or nationality *always* follow the noun (→ **2**)

● As in English, demonstrative, possessive, numerical and interrogative adjectives precede the noun (→ **3**)

● The adjectives **autre** *other* and **chaque** *each, every* precede the noun (→ **4**)

● The following common adjectives can precede the noun:

| | | | |
|---|---|---|---|
| **beau** | *beautiful* | **jeune** | *young* |
| **bon** | *good* | **joli** | *pretty* |
| **court** | *short* | **long** | *long* |
| **dernier** | *last* | **mauvais** | *bad* |
| **grand** | *great* | **petit** | *small* |
| **gros** | *big* | **tel** | *such (a)* |
| **haut** | *high* | **vieux** | *old* |

● The meaning of the following adjectives varies according to their position:

| | BEFORE NOUN | AFTER NOUN | |
|---|---|---|---|
| **ancien** | *former* | *old, ancient* | (→ **5**) |
| **brave** | *good* | *brave* | (→ **6**) |
| **cher** | *dear (beloved)* | *expensive* | (→ **7**) |
| **grand** | *great* | *tall* | (→ **8**) |
| **même** | *same* | *very* | (→ **9**) |
| **pauvre** | *poor (wretched)* | *poor (not rich)* | (→ **10**) |
| **propre** | *own* | *clean* | (→ **11**) |
| **seul** | *single, sole* | *on one's own* | (→ **12**) |
| **simple** | *mere, simple* | *simple, easy* | (→ **13**) |
| **vrai** | *real* | *true* | (→ **14**) |

● Adjectives following the noun are linked by **et** (→ **15**)

1 **le chapitre** suivant
the following chapter

**l'heure** exacte
the right time

2 **une cravate** rouge
a red tie

**un mot** français
a French word

3 **ce dictionnaire**
this dictionary

**mon père**
my father

**le** premier **étage**
the first floor

**deux exemples**
two examples

**quel homme?**
which man?

4 **une** autre **fois**
another time

**chaque jour**
every day

5 **un** ancien **collègue**
a former colleague

**l'histoire** ancienne
ancient history

6 **un** brave **homme**
a good man

**un homme** brave
a brave man

7 **mes** chers **amis**
my dear friends

**une robe** chère
an expensive dress

8 **un** grand **peintre**
a great painter

**un homme** grand
a tall man

9 **la** même **réponse**
the same answer

**vos paroles** mêmes
your very words

10 **cette** pauvre **femme**
that poor woman

**une nation** pauvre
a poor nation

11 **ma** propre **vie**
my own life

**une chemise** propre
a clean shirt

12 **une** seule **réponse**
a single reply

**une femme** seule
a woman on her own

13 **un** simple **regard**
a mere look

**un problème** simple
a simple problem

14 **la** vraie **raison**
the real reason

**les faits** vrais
the true facts

15 **un acte lâche** et **trompeur**
a cowardly, deceitful act

**un acte lâche, trompeur** et **ignoble**
a cowardly, deceitful and ignoble act

## Personal Pronouns

*SUBJECT PRONOUNS*

| PERSON | SINGULAR | PLURAL |
|---|---|---|
| 1st | **je (j')** | **nous** |
| | *I* | *we* |
| 2nd | **tu** | **vous** |
| | *you* | *you* |
| 3rd (masc.) | **il** | **ils** |
| | *he; it* | *they* |
| (fem.) | **elle** | **elles** |
| | *she; it* | *they* |

**je** changes to **j'** before a vowel, an **h** 'mute', or the pronoun **y** (→ **1**)

● **tu/vous**
 **Vous**, as well as being the second person plural, is also used when addressing one person. As a general rule, use **tu** only when addressing a friend, a child, a relative, someone you know very well, or when invited to do so. In all other cases use **vous**. For singular and plural uses of **vous**, see example **2**.

● **il/elle; ils/elles**
 The form of the 3rd person pronouns reflects the number and gender of the noun(s) they replace, referring to animals and things as well as to people. **Ils** also replaces a combination of masculine and feminine nouns (→ **3**)

● Sometimes stressed pronouns replace the subject pronouns, see p. 172

*Continued*

**1 J'arrive!**
I'm just coming!
**J'en ai trois**
I've got 3 of them
**J'hésite à le déranger**
I hesitate to disturb him
**J'y pense souvent**
I often think about it

**2** Compare:    **Vous êtes certain, Monsieur Leclerc?**
Are you sure, Mr Leclerc?
and:    **Vous êtes certains, les enfants?**
Are you sure, children?
Compare:    **Vous êtes partie quand, Estelle?**
When did you leave, Estelle?
and:    **Estelle et Sophie – vous êtes parties quand?**
Estelle and Sophie – when did you leave?

**3 Où logent ton père et ta mère quand ils vont à Rome?**
Where do your father and mother stay when they go to Rome?
**Donne-moi le journal et les lettres quand ils arriveront**
Give me the newspaper and the letters when they arrive

## Personal Pronouns (ctd.)

*DIRECT OBJECT PRONOUNS*

| PERSON | SINGULAR | PLURAL |
|---|---|---|
| 1st | **me (m')** | **nous** |
| | *me* | *us* |
| 2nd | **te (t')** | **vous** |
| | *you* | *you* |
| 3rd (masc.) | **le (l')** | **les** |
| | *him; it* | *them* |
| (fem.) | **la (l')** | **les** |
| | *her; it* | *them* |

The forms shown in brackets are used before a vowel, an **h** 'mute', or the pronoun **y** (→ **1**)

● In positive commands **me** and **te** change to **moi** and **toi** except before **en** or **y** (→ **2**)

● **le** sometimes functions as a 'neuter' pronoun, referring to an idea or information contained in a previous statement or question. It is often not translated (→ **3**)

**Position of direct object pronouns**
● In constructions other than the imperative affirmative the pronoun comes before the verb (→ **4**)
The same applies when the verb is in the infinitive (→ **5**)
In the imperative affirmative, the pronoun follows the verb and is attached to it by a hyphen (→ **6**)

● For further information, see Order of Object Pronouns, p. 170

**Reflexive Pronouns**
These are dealt with under reflexive verbs, p. 30

*Continued*

**1 Il m'a vu**
He saw me
**Je ne t'oublierai jamais**
I'll never forget you
**Ça l'habitue à travailler seul**
That gets him/her used to working on his/her own
**Je veux l'y accoutumer**
I want to accustom him/her to it

**2 Avertis-moi de ta décision** → **Avertis-m'en**
Inform me of your decision    Inform me of it

**3 Il n'est pas là. – Je le sais bien.**
He isn't there. – I know that.
**Aidez-moi si vous le pouvez**
Help me if you can
**Elle viendra demain. – Je l'espère bien.**
She'll come tomorrow. – I hope so.

**4 Je t'aime**
I love you
**Les voyez-vous?**
Can you see them?
**Elle ne nous connaît pas**
She doesn't know us
**Est-ce que tu ne les aimes pas?**
Don't you like them?
**Ne me faites pas rire**
Don't make me laugh

**5 Puis-je vous aider?**
May I help you?

**6 Aidez-moi**                    **Suivez-nous**
Help me                          Follow us

## Personal Pronouns (ctd.)

*INDIRECT OBJECT PRONOUNS*

| PERSON | SINGULAR | PLURAL |
|---|---|---|
| 1st | **me (m')** | **nous** |
| 2nd | **te (t')** | **vous** |
| 3rd (masc.) | **lui** | **leur** |
| (fem.) | **lui** | **leur** |

**me** and **te** change to **m'** and **t'** before a vowel or an **h** 'mute'
(→1)

● In positive commands, **me** and **te** change to **moi** and **toi** except
before **en** (→2)

● The pronouns shown in the above table replace the preposition **à** +
noun, where the noun is a person or an animal (→3)

● The verbal construction affects the translation of the pronoun (→4)

**Position of indirect object pronouns**
● In constructions other than the imperative affirmative, the pronoun
comes before the verb (→5)
The same applies when the verb is in the infinitive (→6)
In the imperative affirmative, the pronoun follows the verb and is
attached to it by a hyphen (→7)

● For further information, see Order of Object Pronouns, p. 170

**Reflexive Pronouns**
These are dealt with under reflexive verbs, p. 30

*Continued*

1 **Tu m'as donné ce livre**
You gave me this book
**Ils t'ont caché les faits**
They hid the facts from you

2 **Donnez-moi du sucre**    → **Donnez-m'en**
Give me some sugar         Give me some
**Garde-toi assez d'argent**  → **Garde-t'en assez**
Keep enough money for      Keep enough for yourself
yourself

3 **J'écris à Suzanne**     → **Je lui écris**
I'm writing to Suzanne       I'm writing to her
**Donne du lait au chat**   → **Donne-lui du lait**
Give the cat some milk        Give it some milk

4 **arracher qch à qn**   to snatch sth from sb:
    **Un voleur m'a arraché mon porte-monnaie**
    A thief snatched my purse from me
**promettre qch à qn**   to promise sb sth:
    **Il leur a promis un cadeau**
    He promised them a present
**demander à qn de faire**   to ask sb to do:
    **Elle nous avait demandé de revenir**
    She had asked us to come back

5 **Elle vous a écrit**             **Vous a-t-elle écrit?**
She's written to you           Has she written to you?
**Il ne nous parle pas**
He doesn't speak to us
**Est-ce que cela ne vous intéresse pas?**
Doesn't it interest you?
**Ne leur répondez pas**
Don't answer them

6 **Voulez-vous leur envoyer l'adresse?**
Do you want to send them the address?

7 **Répondez-moi**           **Donnez-nous la réponse**
Answer me                 Tell us the answer

## Personal Pronouns (ctd.)

**Order of object pronouns**

● When two object pronouns of different persons come before the verb, the order is: indirect before direct, i.e.

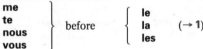

$$\left.\begin{array}{l} \textbf{me} \\ \textbf{te} \\ \textbf{nous} \\ \textbf{vous} \end{array}\right\} \text{ before } \left\{\begin{array}{l} \textbf{le} \\ \textbf{la} \\ \textbf{les} \end{array}\right. \quad (\rightarrow 1)$$

● When two 3rd person object pronouns come before the verb, the order is: direct before indirect, i.e.

$$\left.\begin{array}{l} \textbf{le} \\ \textbf{la} \\ \textbf{les} \end{array}\right\} \text{ before } \left\{\begin{array}{l} \textbf{lui} \\ \textbf{leur} \end{array}\right. \quad (\rightarrow 2)$$

● When two object pronouns come after the verb (i.e. in the imperative affirmative), the order is: direct before indirect, i.e.

$$\left.\begin{array}{l} \textbf{le} \\ \textbf{la} \\ \textbf{les} \end{array}\right\} \text{ before } \left\{\begin{array}{l} \textbf{moi} \\ \textbf{toi} \\ \textbf{lui} \\ \textbf{nous} \\ \textbf{vous} \\ \textbf{leur} \end{array}\right. \quad (\rightarrow 3)$$

● The pronouns **y** and **en** (see pp. 176 and 174) always come last (→ **4**)

*Continued*

1 **Dominique vous l'envoie demain**
Dominique's sending it to you tomorrow
**Est-ce qu'il te les a montrés?**
Has he shown them to you?
**Ne me le dis pas**
Don't tell me (it)
**Il ne veut pas nous la prêter**
He won't lend it to us

2 **Elle le leur a emprunté**
She borrowed it from them
**Je les lui ai lus**
I read them to him/her
**Ne la leur donne pas**
Don't give it to them
**Je voudrais les lui rendre**
I'd like to give them back to him/her

3 **Rends-les-moi**
Give them back to me
**Donnez-le-nous**
Give it to us
**Apportons-les-leur**
Let's take them to them

4 **Donnez-leur-en**
Give them some
**Je l'y ai déposé**
I dropped him there
**Ne nous en parlez plus**
Don't speak to us about it any more

## Personal Pronouns (ctd.)

*STRESSED OR DISJUNCTIVE PRONOUNS*

| PERSON | SINGULAR | PLURAL |
|---|---|---|
| 1st | **moi** | **nous** |
| | *me* | *us* |
| 2nd | **toi** | **vous** |
| | *you* | *you* |
| 3rd (masc.) | **lui** | **eux** |
| | *him; it* | *them* |
| (fem.) | **elle** | **elles** |
| | *her; it* | *them* |
| ('reflexive') | **soi** | |
| | *oneself* | |

● These pronouns are used:
  – after prepositions (→ **1**)
  – on their own (→ **2**)
  – following **c'est**, **ce sont** *it is* (→ **3**)
  – for emphasis, especially where contrast is involved (→ **4**)
  – when the subject consists of two or more pronouns (→ **5**)
  – when the subject consists of a pronoun and a noun (→ **6**)
  – in comparisons (→ **7**)
  – before relative pronouns (→ **8**)

● For particular emphasis **-même** (singular) or **-mêmes** (plural) is
  added to the pronoun (→ **9**)

| | | | |
|---|---|---|---|
| **moi-même** | *myself* | **nous-mêmes** | *ourselves* |
| **toi-même** | *yourself* | **vous-même** | *yourself* |
| **lui-même** | *himself; itself* | **vous-mêmes** | *yourselves* |
| **elle-même** | *herself; itself* | **eux-mêmes** | *themselves* |
| **soi-même** | *oneself* | **elles-mêmes** | *themselves* |

1 **Je pense à toi**
I think about you
**C'est pour elle**
This is for her
**Venez avec moi**
Come with me

**Partez sans eux**
Leave without them
**Assieds-toi à côté de lui**
Sit beside him
**Il a besoin de nous**
He needs us

2 **Qui a fait cela? – Lui.**
Who did that? – He did.
**Qui est-ce qui gagne? – Moi**
Who's winning? – Me

3 **C'est toi, Simon? – Non, c'est moi, David.**
Is that you, Simon? – No, it's me, David
**Qui est-ce? – Ce sont eux.**
Who is it? – It's them.

4 **Ils voyagent séparément: lui par le train, elle en autobus**
They travel separately: he by train and she by bus
**Toi, tu ressembles à ton père, eux pas**
*You* look like your father, *they* don't
**Il n'a pas l'air de s'ennuyer, lui!**
*He* doesn't look bored!

5 **Lui et moi partons demain**
He and I are leaving tomorrow
**Ni vous ni elles ne pouvez rester**
Neither you nor they can stay

6 **Mon père et elle ne s'entendent pas**
My father and she don't get on

7 **plus jeune que moi**
younger than me
**Il est moins grand que toi**
He's smaller than you (are)

8 **Moi, qui étais malade, je n'ai pas pu les accompagner**
I, who was ill, couldn't go with them
**Ce sont eux qui font du bruit, pas nous**
They're the ones making the noise, not us

9 **Je l'ai fait moi-même**
I did it myself

## The pronoun en

● **en** replaces the preposition **de** + noun (→ **1**)
The verbal construction can affect the translation (→ **2**)

● **en** also replaces the partitive article (*English = some, any*) + noun
(→ **3**)

In expressions of quantity **en** represents the noun (→ **4**)

● Position:
**en** comes before the verb, except in positive commands when it
follows and is attached to the verb by a hyphen (→ **5**)

● **en** follows other object pronouns (→ **6**)

**1** **Il est fier de son succès** → **Il en est fier**
He's proud of his success      He's proud of it
**Elle est sortie du cinéma** → **Elle en est sortie**
She came out of the cinema    She came out (of it)
**Je suis couvert de peinture** → **J'en suis couvert**
I'm covered in paint        I'm covered in it
**Il a beaucoup d'amis** → **Il en a beaucoup**
He has lots of friends      He has lots (of them)

**2** **avoir besoin de qch**   to need sth:
     **J'en ai besoin**
     I need it/them
**avoir peur de qch**   to be afraid of sth:
     **J'en ai peur**
     I'm afraid of it/them

**3** **Avez-vous de l'argent?** → **En avez-vous?**
Have you any money?      Do you have any?
**Je veux acheter des timbres** → **Je veux en acheter**
I want to buy some stamps    I want to buy some

**4** **J'ai deux crayons** → **J'en ai deux**
I've two pencils      I've two (of them)
**Combien de sœurs as-tu? – J'en ai trois.**
How many sisters do you have? – I have three.

**5** **Elle en a discuté avec moi**
She discussed it with me
**En êtes-vous content?**
Are you pleased with
it/them?
**Je veux en garder trois**
I want to keep three of them
**N'en parlez plus**
Don't talk about it any more
**Prenez-en**             **Soyez-en fier**
Take some             Be proud of it/them

**6** **Donnez-leur-en**        **Il m'en a parlé**
Give them some        He spoke to me about it

## The pronoun y

● **y** replaces the preposition **à** + noun (→ **1**)
   The verbal construction can affect the translation (→ **2**)

● **y** also replaces the prepositions **dans** and **sur** + noun (→ **3**)

● **y** can also mean *there* (→ **4**)

● Position:
   **y** comes before the verb, except in positive commands when it
   follows and is attached to the verb by a hyphen (→ **5**)

● **y** follows other object pronouns (→ **6**)

**1 Ne touchez pas à ce bouton** → **N'y touchez pas**
Don't touch this switch            Don't touch it
**Il participe aux concerts** → **Il y participe**
He takes part in the concerts     He takes part (in them)

**2 penser à qch**   to think about sth:
   **J'y pense souvent**
   I often think about it
**consentir à qch**   to agree to sth:
   **Tu y as consenti?**
   Have you agreed to it?

**3 Mettez-les dans la boîte** → **Mettez-les-y**
Put them in the box               Put them in it
**Il les a mis sur les étagères** → **Il les y a mis**
He put them on the shelves        He put them on them
**J'ai placé de l'argent sur ce
compte**                           → **J'y ai placé de l'argent**
I've put money into this           I've put money into it
account

**4 Elle y passe tout l'été**
She spends the whole summer there

**5 Il y a ajouté du sucre**
He added sugar to it
**Elle n'y a pas écrit son nom**
She hasn't written her name on it
**Comment fait-on pour y aller?**
How do you get there?
**N'y pense plus!**
Don't give it another thought!
**Restez-y**                        **Réfléchissez-y**
Stay there                          Think it over

**6 Elle m'y a conduit**            **Menez-nous-y**
She drove me there                  Take us there

## Indefinite Pronouns

| | | |
|---|---|---|
| aucun(e) | *none, not any* | (→1) |
| certain(e)s | *some, certain* | (→2) |
| chacun(e) | *each (one)* *everybody* | (→3) |
| on | *one, you* *somebody* *they, people* *we* (informal use) | (→4) |
| personne | *nobody* | (→5) |
| plusieurs | *several* | (→6) |
| quelque chose | *something; anything* | (→7) |
| quelques-un(e)s | *some, a few* | (→8) |
| quelqu'un | *somebody; anybody* | (→9) |
| rien | *nothing* | (→10) |
| tout | *all; everything* | (→11) |
| tous (toutes) | *all* | (→12) |
| l'un(e) ... l'autre | *(the) one ... the other* | |
| les un(e)s ... les autres | *some ...others* | (→13) |

● **aucun(e), personne, rien**

When used as subject or object of the verb, these require the word **ne** placed immediately before the verb. Note that **aucun** further needs the pronoun **en** when used as an object ( →14)

● **quelque chose, rien**

When qualified by an adjective, these pronouns require the preposition **de** before the adjective ( →15)

1 **Combien en avez-vous? – Aucun**
How many have you got? – None

2 **Certains pensent que ...**
Some (people) think that ...

3 **Chacune de ces boîtes est pleine**     **Chacun son tour!**
Each of these boxes is full              Everybody in turn!

4 **On voit l'église de cette fenêtre**
You can see the church from this window
**À la campagne on se couche tôt**
In the country they/we go to bed early
**Est-ce qu'on lui a permis de rester?**
Was he/she allowed to stay?

5 **Qui voyez-vous? – Personne**
Who can you see? – Nobody

6 **Ils sont plusieurs**
There are several of them

7 **Mange donc quelque chose!**          **Tu as vu quelque chose?**
Eat something!                          Did you see anything?

8 **Je connais quelques-uns de ses amis**
I know some of his/her friends

9 **Quelqu'un a appelé**                 **Tu as vu quelqu'un?**
Somebody called (out)                   Did you see anybody?

10 **Qu'est-ce que tu as dans la main? – Rien**
What have you got in your hand? – Nothing

11 **Il a tout gâché**                   **Tout va bien**
He has spoiled everything               All's well

12 **Tu les as tous?**                   **Elles sont toutes venues**
Do you have all of them?                They all came

13 **Les uns sont satisfaits, les autres pas**
Some are satisfied, (the) others aren't

14 **Je ne vois personne**              **Rien ne lui plaît**
I can't see anyone                      Nothing pleases him/her
**Aucune des entreprises ne veut ...**  **Il n'en a aucun**
None of the companies wants ...         He hasn't any (of them)

15 **quelque chose de grand**           **rien d'intéressant**
something big                           nothing interesting

## Relative Pronouns

**qui** *who; which*
**que** *who(m); which*

These are subject and direct object pronouns that introduce a clause and refer to people or things.

|  | PEOPLE | THINGS |
|---|---|---|
| SUBJECT | **qui** (→1) | **qui** (→3) |
|  | *who, that* | *which, that* |
| DIRECT OBJECT | **que (qu')** (→2) | **que (qu')** (→4) |
|  | *who(m), that* | *which, that* |

● **que** changes to **qu'** before a vowel (→2/4)
● You cannot omit the object relative pronoun in French as you can in English (→2/4)

After a preposition:
● When referring to people, use **qui** (→5)
   Exceptions: after **parmi** *among* and **entre** *between* use **lesquels/lesquelles** (see below) (→6)
● When referring to things, use forms of **lequel**:

|  | MASCULINE | FEMININE |  |
|---|---|---|---|
| SING. | **lequel** | **laquelle** | *which* |
| PLUR. | **lesquels** | **lesquelles** | *which* |

   The pronoun agrees in number and gender with the noun (→7)

● After the prepositions **à** and **de, lequel** and **lesquel(le)s** contract as follows:

> **à + lequel → auquel**
> **à + lesquels → auxquels**          (→8)
> **à + lesquelles → auxquelles**
>
> **de + lequel → duquel**
> **de + lesquels → desquels**          (→9)
> **de + lesquelles → desquelles**

*Continued*

**1 Mon frère, qui a vingt ans, est à l'université**
My brother, who's twenty, is at university

**2 Les amis que je vois le plus sont …**
The friends (that) I see most are …
**Lucienne, qu'il connaît depuis longtemps, est …**
Lucienne, whom he has known for a long time, is …

**3 Il y a un escalier qui mène au toit**
There's a staircase which leads to the roof

**4 La maison que nous avons achetée a …**
The house (which) we've bought has …
**Voici le cadeau qu'elle m'a envoyé**
This is the present (that) she sent me

**5 la personne à qui il parle**
the person he's talking to
**la personne avec qui je voyage**
the person with whom I travel
**les enfants pour qui je l'ai acheté**
the children for whom I bought it

**6 Il y avait des jeunes, parmi lesquels Robert**
There were some young people, Robert among them
**les filles entre lesquelles j'étais assis**
the girls between whom I was sitting

**7 le torchon avec lequel il l'essuie**
the cloth he's wiping it with
**la table sur laquelle je l'ai mis**
the table on which I put it
**les moyens par lesquels il l'accomplit**
the means by which he achieves it
**les pièces pour lesquelles elle est connue**
the plays for which she is famous

**8 le magasin auquel il livre ces marchandises**
the shop to which he delivers these goods

**9 les injustices desquelles il se plaint**
the injustices he's complaining about

## Relative Pronouns (ctd.)

**quoi**    *which, what*

● When the relative pronoun does not refer to a specific noun, **quoi** is used after a preposition (→**1**)

**dont**    *whose, of whom, of which*

● **dont** often (but not always) replaces **de qui, duquel, de laquelle,** and **desquel(le)s** (→**2**)

● It cannot replace **de qui, duquel** etc in the construction preposition + noun + **de qui/duquel** (→**3**)

*Continued*

**1 C'est en quoi vous vous trompez**
That's where you're wrong
**A quoi, j'ai répondu '…'**
To which I replied, '…'

**2 la femme dont (= de qui) la voiture est garée en face**
the woman whose car is parked opposite
**un prix dont (= de qui) je suis fier**
an award I am proud of
**un ami dont (= de qui) je connais le frère**
a friend whose brother I know
**les enfants dont (= de qui) vous vous occupez**
the children you look after
**le film dont (= duquel) il a parlé**
the film of which he spoke
**la fenêtre dont (= de laquelle) les rideaux sont tirés**
the window whose curtains are drawn
**des livres dont (= desquels) j'ai oublié les titres**
books whose titles I've forgotten
**les maladies dont (= desquelles) il souffre**
the illnesses he suffers from

**3 une personne sur l'aide de qui on peut compter**
a person whose help one can rely on
**les enfants aux parents de qui j'écris**
the children to whose parents I'm writing
**la maison dans le jardin de laquelle il y a …**
the house in whose garden there is …

## Relative Pronouns (ctd.)

**ce qui, ce que**   *that which, what*
These are used when the relative pronoun does not refer to a specific
noun, and they are often translated as *what* (literally: *that which*)

> **ce qui**      is used as the subject (→**1**)
> **ce que***     is used as the direct object (→**2**)
>
> ***que** changes to **qu'** before a vowel (→**2**)

● Note the construction

> **tout ce qui**  } *everything/all that*   (→**3**)
> **tout ce que**  }

● **de + ce que → ce dont** (→**4**)

● preposition + **ce que** → **ce** + preposition + **quoi** (→**5**)

● When **ce qui**, **ce que** etc, refers to a previous CLAUSE the
  translation is *which* (→**6**)

*Continued*

**1 Ce qui m'intéresse ne l'intéresse pas forcément**
What interests me doesn't necessarily interest him
**Je n'ai pas vu ce qui s'est passé**
I didn't see what happened

**2 Ce que j'aime c'est la musique classique**
What I like is classical music
**Montrez-moi ce qu'il vous a donné**
Show me what he gave you

**3 Tout ce qui reste c'est ...**
All that's left is ...
**Donnez-moi tout ce que vous avez**
Give me everything you have

**4 Il risque de perdre ce dont il est si fier**
He risks losing what he's so proud of
**Voilà ce dont il s'agit**
That's what it's about

**5 Ce n'est pas ce à quoi je m'attendais**
It's not what I was expecting
**Ce à quoi je m'intéresse particulièrement c'est ...**
What I'm particularly interested in is ...

**6 Il est d'accord, ce qui m'étonne**
He agrees, which surprises me
**Il a dit qu'elle ne venait pas, ce que nous savions déjà**
He said she wasn't coming, which we already knew

## Interrogative Pronouns

**qui?** *who?; whom?*
**que?** *what?*
**quoi?** *what?*

These pronouns are used in direct questions.
The form of the pronoun depends on:
>   – whether it refers to people or to things
>   – whether it is the subject or object of the verb, or if it comes
>     after a preposition

**Qui** and **que** have longer forms, as shown in the tables below.

● Referring to people:

| | | |
|---|---|---|
| SUBJECT | **qui?** | |
| | **qui est-ce qui?** | (→1) |
| | *who?* | |
| OBJECT | **qui?** | |
| | **qui est-ce que\*?** | (→2) |
| | *who(m)?* | |
| AFTER PREPOSITIONS | **qui?** | (→3) |
| | *who(m)?* | |

● Referring to things:

| | | |
|---|---|---|
| SUBJECT | **qu'est-ce qui?** | (→4) |
| | *what?* | |
| OBJECT | **que\*?** | |
| | **qu'est-ce que\*?** | (→5) |
| | *what?* | |
| AFTER PREPOSITIONS | **quoi?** | (→6) |
| | *what?* | |

**\*que** changes to **qu'** before a vowel (→2, 5)

*Continued*

1 **Qui vient?**
   **Qui est-ce qui vient?**
   Who's coming?

2 **Qui vois-tu?**
   **Qui est-ce que tu vois?**
   Who(m) can you see?
   **Qui a-t-elle rencontré?**
   **Qui est-ce qu'elle a rencontré?**
   Who(m) did she meet?

3 **De qui parle-t-il?**
   Who's he talking about?
   **Pour qui est ce livre?**
   Who's this book for?
   **A qui avez-vous écrit?**
   To whom did you write?

4 **Qu'est-ce qui se passe?**
   What's happening?
   **Qu'est-ce qui a vexé Paul?**
   What upset Paul?

5 **Que faites-vous?**
   **Qu'est-ce que vous faites?**
   What are you doing?
   **Qu'a-t-il dit?**
   **Qu'est-ce qu'il a dit?**
   What did he say?

6 **A quoi cela sert-il?**
   What's that used for?
   **De quoi a-t-on parlé?**
   What was the discussion about?
   **Sur quoi vous basez-vous?**
   What do you base it on?

## Interrogative Pronouns (ctd.)

**qui**   *who; whom*
**ce qui**   *what*
**ce que**   *what*
**quoi**   *what*

These pronouns are used in indirect questions.
The form of the pronoun depends on:

> – whether it refers to people or to things
> – whether it is the subject or object of the verb, or if it comes
>   after a preposition

● Referring to people: use **qui** in all instances (→**1**)

● Referring to things:

| | | |
|---|---|---|
| *SUBJECT* | **ce qui**<br>*what* | (→**2**) |
| *OBJECT* | **ce que**\*<br>*what* | (→**3**) |
| *AFTER*<br>*PREPOSITIONS* | **quoi**<br>*what* | (→**4**) |

\***que** changes to **qu'** before a vowel (→**3**)

*Continued*

1 **Demande-lui qui est venu**
Ask him who came
**Je me demande qui ils ont vu**
I wonder who they saw
**Dites-moi qui vous préférez**
Tell me who you prefer
**Elle ne sait pas à qui s'adresser**
She doesn't know who to apply to
**Demandez-leur pour qui elles travaillent**
Ask them who they work for

2 **Il se demande ce qui se passe**
He's wondering what's happening
**Je ne sais pas ce qui vous fait croire que ...**
I don't know what makes you think that ...

3 **Raconte-nous ce que tu as fait**
Tell us what you did
**Je me demande ce qu'elle pense**
I wonder what she's thinking

4 **On ne sait pas de quoi vivent ces animaux**
We don't know what these animals live on
**Je vais lui demander à quoi il fait allusion**
I'm going to ask him what he's hinting at

## Interrogative Pronouns (ctd.)

**lequel?, laquelle?; lesquels?, lesquelles?**

|  | MASCULINE | FEMININE |  |
|---|---|---|---|
| SING. | **lequel?** | **laquelle?** | which (one)? |
| PLUR. | **lesquels?** | **lesquelles?** | which (ones)? |

● The pronoun agrees in number and gender with the noun it refers to (→1)

● The same forms are used in indirect questions (→2)

● After the prepositions à and de, **lequel** and **lesquel(le)s** contract as follows:

> à + lequel? → auquel?
> à + lesquels? → auxquels?
> à + lesquelles? → auxquelles?
>
> de + lequel? → duquel?
> de + lesquels? → desquels?
> de + lesquelles? → desquelles?

1 **J'ai choisi un livre. – Lequel?**
   I've chosen a book. – Which one?
   **Laquelle de ces valises est la vôtre?**
   Which of these cases is yours?
   **Amenez quelques amis. – Lesquels?**
   Bring some friends. – Which ones?
   **Lesquelles de vos sœurs sont mariées?**
   Which of your sisters are married?

2 **Je me demande laquelle des maisons est la leur**
   I wonder which is their house
   **Dites-moi lesquels d'entre eux étaient là**
   Tell me which of them were there

## Possessive Pronouns

| | SINGULAR | |
|---|---|---|
| *MASCULINE* | *FEMININE* | |
| **le mien** | **la mienne** | *mine* |
| **le tien** | **la tienne** | *yours* |
| **le sien** | **la sienne** | *his; hers; its* |
| **le nôtre** | **la nôtre** | *ours* |
| **le vôtre** | **la vôtre** | *yours* |
| **le leur** | **la leur** | *theirs* |

| | PLURAL | |
|---|---|---|
| *MASCULINE* | *FEMININE* | |
| **les miens** | **les miennes** | *mine* |
| **les tiens** | **les tiennes** | *yours* |
| **les siens** | **les siennes** | *his; hers; its* |
| **les nôtres** | **les nôtres** | *ours* |
| **les vôtres** | **les vôtres** | *yours* |
| **les leurs** | **les leurs** | *theirs* |

● The pronoun agrees in number and gender with the noun it replaces, NOT WITH THE OWNER (→1)

● Alternative translations are *my own, your own* etc; **le sien, la sienne** etc. may also mean *one's own* (→2)

● After the prepositions **à** and **de** the articles **le** and **les** are contracted in the normal way (see p. 140):

> **à + le mien → au mien**
> **à + les miens → aux miens**            (→3)
> **à + les miennes → aux miennes**
>
> **de + le mien → du mien**
> **de + les miens → des miens**            (→4)
> **de + les miennes → des miennes**

**1** **Demandez à Carole si ce stylo est** le sien
Ask Carol if this pen is hers
**Quelle équipe a gagné –** la leur **ou** la nôtre?
Which team won – theirs or ours?
**Mon stylo marche mieux que** le tien
My pen writes better than yours
**Richard a pris mes affaires pour** les siennes
Richard mistook my belongings for his
**Si tu n'as pas de disques, emprunte** les miens
If you don't have any records, borrow mine
**Nos maisons sont moins grandes que** les vôtres
Our houses are smaller than yours

**2** **Est-ce que leur entreprise est aussi grande que** la vôtre?
Is their company as big as your own?
**Leurs prix sont moins élevés que** les nôtres
Their prices are lower than our own
**Le bonheur des autres importe plus que** le sien
Other people's happiness matters more than one's own

**3** **Pourquoi préfères-tu ce manteau** au mien?
Why do you prefer this coat to mine?
**Quelles maisons ressemblent** aux leurs?
Which houses resemble theirs?

**4** Leur **car est garé**
Their coach is parked
**Vos livres sont au-dessus** des miens
Your books are on top of mine

## Demonstrative Pronouns

**celui, celle; ceux, celles**

|  | MASCULINE | FEMININE |  |
|---|---|---|---|
| SING. | celui | celle | the one |
| PLUR. | ceux | celles | the ones |

● The pronoun agrees in number and gender with the noun it replaces
  (→1)

● Uses:
  – preceding a relative pronoun, meaning *the one(s) who/which*
    (→1)
  – preceding the preposition **de**, meaning *the one(s) belonging to,
    the one(s) of* (→2)
  – with **-ci** and **-là**, for emphasis or to distinguish between two things:

|  | MASCULINE | FEMININE |  |  |
|---|---|---|---|---|
| SING. | celui-ci | celle-ci | *this (one)* | (→3) |
| PLUR. | ceux-ci | celles-ci | *these (ones)* | |

|  | MASCULINE | FEMININE |  |  |
|---|---|---|---|---|
| SING. | celui-là | celle-là | *that (one)* | (→3) |
| PLUR. | ceux-là | celles-là | *those (ones)* | |

  – an additional meaning of **celui-ci/celui-là** etc. is *the former/the
    latter*

*Continued*

1 **Lequel? – Celui qui parle à Anne**
Which man? – The one who's talking to Anne
**Quelle robe désirez-vous? – Celle qui est en vitrine**
Which dress do you want? – The one which is in the window
**Est-ce que ces livres sont ceux qu'il t'a donnés?**
Are these the books that he gave you?
**Quelles filles? – Celles que nous avons vues hier**
Which girls? – The ones we saw yesterday
**Cet article n'est pas celui dont vous m'avez parlé**
This article isn't the one you spoke to me about

2 **Ce jardin est plus grand que celui de mes parents**
This garden is bigger than my parents' (garden)
**Est-ce que ta fille est plus âgée que celle de Gabrielle?**
Is your daughter older than Gabrielle's (daughter)?
**Je préfère les enfants de Paul à ceux de Roger**
I prefer Paul's children to Roger's (children)
**Comparez vos réponses à celles de votre voisin**
Compare your answers with your neighbours (answers)
**les montagnes d'Écosse et celles du pays de Galles**
the mountains of Scotland and those of Wales

3 **Quel tailleur préférez-vous: celui-ci ou celui-là?**
Which suit do you prefer: this one or that one?
**Cette chemise a deux poches mais celle-là n'en a pas**
This shirt has two pockets but that one has none
**Quels œufs choisirais-tu: ceux-ci ou ceux-là?**
Which eggs would you choose: these (ones) or those (ones)?
**De toutes mes jupes, celle-ci me va le mieux**
Of all my skirts, this one fits me best

## Demonstrative Pronouns (ctd.)

**ce (c')**   *it, that*

● Usually used with **être**, in the expressions **c'est**, **c'était**, **ce sont** etc. (→**1**)

● Note the spelling **ç** when followed by the letter **a** (→**2**)

● Uses:
  – to identify a person or object (→**3**)
  – for emphasis (→**4**)
  – as a neuter pronoun, referring to a statement, idea etc. (→**5**)

**ce qui, ce que, ce dont** etc.: see Relative Pronouns (p. 184), Interrogative Pronouns (p. 188)

**cela, ça**   *it, that*

● **cela** and **ça** are used as 'neuter' pronouns, referring to a statement, an idea, an object (→**6**)

● In everyday spoken language **ça** is used in preference to **cela**

**ceci**   *this* (→**7**)

● **ceci** is not used as often as 'this' in English; **cela**, **ça** are often used where we use 'this'

1 **C'est ...**
   It's/That's ...
   **C'était moi**
   It was me

2 **Ç'a été la cause de ...**
   It has been cause of ...

3 **Qui est-ce?**
   Who is it?; Who's this/that?; Who's he/she?
   **C'est lui/mon frère/nous**
   It's/That's him/my brother/us
   **Ce sont eux**
   It's them
   **C'est une infirmière***
   She's a nurse
   **Ce sont des professeurs***
   They're teachers
   **Qu'est-ce que c'est?**
   What's this/that?
   **Qu'est-ce que c'est que ça?**
   What's that?
   **C'est une agrafeuse**
   It's a stapler
   **Ce sont des trombones**
   They're paper clips

4 **C'est moi qui ai téléphoné**
   It was me who phoned
   **Ce sont les enfants qui importent le plus**
   It's the children who matter most

5 **C'est très intéressant**
   That's/It's very interesting
   **Ce serait dangereux**
   That/It would be dangerous

6 **Ça ne fait rien**
   It doesn't matter
   **A quoi bon faire ça?**
   What's the use of doing that?
   **Cela ne compte pas**
   That doesn't count
   **Cela demande du temps**
   It/That takes time

7 **A qui est ceci?**
   Whose is this?
   **Ouvrez-le comme ceci**
   Open it like this

*See pp. 146 and 147 for the use of the article when stating a person's profession

## Adverbs

### Formation

- Most adverbs are formed by adding **-ment** to the feminine form of the adjective (→**1**)

- **-ment** is added to the *masculine* form when the masculine form ends in **-é**, **-i** or **-u** (→**2**)
  Exception: **gai** (→**3**)
  Occasionally the **u** changes to **û** before **-ment** is added (→**4**)

- If the adjective ends in **-ant** or **-ent**, the adverb ends in **-amment** or **-emment** (→**5**)
  Exceptions: **lent**, **présent** (→**6**)

### Irregular Adverbs

| ADJECTIVE | | ADVERB | | |
|-----------|--------|--------|-------------|--------|
| **aveugle** | *blind* | **aveuglément** | blindly | |
| **bon** | *good* | **bien** | well | (→**7**) |
| **bref** | *brief* | **brièvement** | briefly | |
| **énorme** | *enormous* | **énormément** | enormously | |
| **exprès** | *express* | **expressément** | expressly | (→**8**) |
| **gentil** | *kind* | **gentiment** | kindly | |
| **mauvais** | *bad* | **mal** | badly | (→**9**) |
| **meilleur** | *better* | **mieux** | better | |
| **pire** | *worse* | **pis** | worse | |
| **précis** | *precise* | **précisément** | precisely | |
| **profond** | *deep* | **profondément** | deeply | (→**10**) |
| **traître** | *treacherous* | **traîtreusement** | treacherously | |

### Adjectives used as adverbs

Certain adjectives are used adverbially. These include: **bas, bon, cher, clair, court, doux, droit, dur, faux, ferme, fort, haut, mauvais** and **net** (→**11**)

**1** *MASC/FEM. ADJECTIVE*  *ADVERB*
**heureux/heureuse** fortunate  **heureusement** fortunately
**franc/franche** frank  **franchement** frankly
**extrême/extrême** extreme  **extrêmement** extremely

**2** *MASC. ADJECTIVE*  *ADVERB*
**désespéré** desperate  **désespérément** desperately
**vrai** true  **vraiment** truly
**résolu** resolute  **résolument** resolutely

**3** **gai** cheerful  **gaiement** *OR* **gaîment** cheerfully

**4** **continu** continuous  **continûment** continuously

**5** **constant** constant  **constamment** constantly
**courant** fluent  **couramment** fluently
**évident** obvious  **évidemment** obviously
**fréquent** frequent  **fréquemment** frequently

**6** **lent** slow  **lentement** slowly
**présent** present  **présentement** presently

**7** **Elle travaille bien**
She works well

**8** **Il a expressément défendu qu'on parte**
He has expressly forbidden us to leave

**9** **Un emploi mal payé**
A badly paid job

**10** **J'ai été profondément ému**
I was deeply moved

**11** **parler bas/haut**
to speak softly/loudly
**coûter cher**
to be expensive
**voir clair**
to see clearly
**travailler dur**
to work hard
**chanter faux**
to sing off key
**sentir bon/mauvais**
to smell nice/horrible

## Position of Adverbs

● When the adverb accompanies a verb in a simple tense, it generally follows the verb (→ **1**)
● When the adverb accompanies a verb in a compound tense, it generally comes between the auxiliary verb and the past participle (→ **2**)
  Some adverbs, however, follow the past participle (→ **3**)
● When the adverb accompanies an adjective or another adverb it generally precedes the adjective/adverb (→ **4**)

## Comparatives of Adverbs

These are formed using the following constructions:

| | | |
|---|---|---|
| **plus . . . (que)** | *more . . . (than)* | (→ **5**) |
| **moins . . . (que)** | *less . . . (than)* | (→ **6**) |
| **aussi . . . que** | *as . . . as* | (→ **7**) |
| **si . . . que\*** | *as . . . as* | (→ **8**) |

\*used mainly after a negative

## Superlatives of Adverbs

These are formed using the following constructions:

| | | |
|---|---|---|
| **le plus . . . (que)** | *the most . . . (that)* | (→ **9**) |
| **le moins . . . (que)** | *the least . . . (that)* | (→ **10**) |

**Adverbs with irregular comparatives/superlatives**

| ADVERB | COMPARATIVE | SUPERLATIVE |
|---|---|---|
| **beaucoup** | **plus** | **le plus** |
| *a lot* | *more* | *(the) most* |
| **bien** | **mieux** | **le mieux** |
| *well* | *better* | *(the) best* |
| **mal** | **pis** OR | **le pis** OR |
| | **plus mal** | **le plus mal** |
| *badly* | *worse* | *(the) worst* |
| **peu** | **moins** | **le moins** |
| *little* | *less* | *(the) least* |

1 **Il dort encore**
He's still asleep

**Je pense souvent à toi**
I often think about you

2 **Ils sont déjà partis**
They've already gone
**J'ai presque fini**
I'm almost finished

**J'ai toujours cru que** ...
I've always thought that ...
**Il a trop mangé**
He's eaten too much

3 **On les a vus partout**
We saw them everywhere

**Elle est revenue hier**
She came back yesterday

4 **un très beau chemisier**
a very nice blouse
**beaucoup plus vite**
much faster

**une femme bien habillée**
a well-dressed woman
**peu souvent**
not very often

5 **plus vite**
more quickly
**Elle chante plus fort que moi**
She sings louder than I do

**plus régulièrement**
more regularly

6 **moins facilement**
less easily

**moins souvent**
less often

**Nous nous voyons moins fréquemment qu'auparavant**
We see each other less frequently than before

7 **Faites-le aussi vite que possible**
Do it as quickly as possible
**Il en sait aussi long que nous**
He knows as much about it as we do

8 **Ce n'est pas si loin que je pensais**
It's not as far as I thought

9 **Marianne court le plus vite**
Marianne runs fastest
**Le plus tôt que je puisse venir c'est samedi**
The earliest that I can come is Saturday

10 **C'est l'auteur que je connais le moins bien**
It's the writer I'm least familiar with

## Common adverbs and their usage

| | | |
|---|---|---|
| **assez** | *enough; quite* | (→ **1**) See also below |
| **aussi** | *also, too; as* | (→ **2**) |
| **autant** | *as much* | (→ **3**) See also below |
| **beaucoup** | *a lot; much* | (→ **4**) See also below |
| **bien** | *well; very* | (→ **5**) See also below |
| | *very much; 'indeed'* | |
| **combien** | *how much; how many* | (→ **6**) See also below |
| **comme** | *how; what* | (→ **7**) |
| **déjà** | *already; before* | (→ **8**) |
| **encore** | *still; yet* | (→ **9**) |
| | *more; even* | |
| **moins** | *less* | (→ **10**) See also below |
| **peu** | *little, not much; not very* | (→ **11**) See also below |
| **plus** | *more* | (→ **12**) See also below |
| **si** | *so; such* | (→ **13**) |
| **tant** | *so much* | (→ **14**) See also below |
| **toujours** | *always; still* | (→ **15**) |
| **trop** | *too much; too* | (→ **16**) See also below |

- **assez, autant, beaucoup, combien** etc. are used in the construction *adverb* + **de** + *noun* with the following meanings:

| | | |
|---|---|---|
| **assez de** | *enough* | (→**17**) |
| **autant de** | *as much; as many* | |
| | *so much; so many* | |
| **beaucoup de** | *a lot of* | |
| **combien de** | *how much; how many* | |
| **moins de** | *less; fewer* | (→**17**) |
| **peu de** | *little, not much; few,* | |
| | *not many* | |
| **plus de** | *more* | |
| **tant de** | *so much; so many* | |
| **trop de** | *too much; too many* | |

- **bien** can be followed by a partitive article (see p. 144) plus a noun to mean *a lot of; a good many* (→ **18**)

1 **Avez-vous assez chaud?**
Are you warm enough?

**Il est assez tard**
It's quite late

2 **Je préfère ça aussi**
I prefer it too

**Elle est aussi grande que moi**
She is as tall as I am

3 **Je voyage autant que lui**
I have as much as him

4 **Tu lis beaucoup?**
Do you read a lot?

**C'est beaucoup plus loin?**
Is it much further?

5 **Bien joué!**
Well played!

**Je suis bien content que ...**
I'm very pleased that ...

**Il s'est bien amusé**
He enjoyed himself very much

**Je l'ai bien fait**
I DID do it

6 **Combien coûte ce livre?**
How much is this book?

**Vous êtes combien?**
How many of you are there?

7 **Comme tu es jolie!**
How pretty you look!

**Comme il fait beau!**
What lovely weather!

8 **Je l'ai déjà fait**
I've already done it

**Êtes-vous déjà allé en France?**
Have you been to France before?

9 **J'en ai encore deux**
I've still got two

**Elle n'est pas encore là**
She isn't there yet

**Encore du café, Alain?**
More coffee, Alain?

**Encore mieux!**
Even better!

10 **Travaillez moins**
Work less

**Je suis moins étonné que toi**
I'm less surprised than you are

11 **Elle mange peu**
She doesn't eat very much

**C'est peu important**
It's not very important

12 **Il se détend plus**
He relaxes more

**Elle est plus timide que Sophie**
She is shyer than Sophie

13 **Simon est si charmant**
Simon is so charming

**une si belle vue**
such a lovely view

14 **Elle l'aime tant** She loves him so much

15 **Il dit toujours ça!**
He always says that!

**Tu le vois toujours?**
Do you still see him?

16 **J'ai trop mangé**
I've eaten too much

**C'est trop cher**
It's too expensive

17 **assez d'argent/de livres**
enough money/books

**moins de temps/d'amis**
less time/fewer friends

18 **bien du mal/des gens** a lot of harm/a good many people

On the following pages you will find some of the most frequent uses of prepositions in French. Particular attention is paid to cases where usage differs markedly from English. It is often difficult to give an English equivalent for French prepositions, since usage *does* vary so much between the two languages.

In the list below, the broad meaning of the preposition is given on the left, with examples of usage following.

Prepositions are dealt with in alphabetical order, except **à**, **de** and **en** which are shown first.

## à

| | | |
|---|---|---|
| *at* | **lancer qch à qn** | *to throw sth at sb* |
| | **il habite à St. Pierre** | *he lives at St. Pierre* |
| | **à 5 francs (la) pièce** | *(at) 5 francs each* |
| | **à 100 km à l'heure** | *at 100 km per hour* |
| *in* | **à la campagne** | *in the country* |
| | **à Londres** | *in London* |
| | **au lit** | *in bed* (also *to bed*) |
| | **un livre à la main** | *with a book in his/her hand* |
| *on* | **un tableau au mur** | *a picture on the wall* |
| *to* | **aller au cinéma** | *to go to the cinema* |
| | **donner qch à qn** | *to give sth to sb* |
| | **le premier/dernier à faire** | *the first/last to do* |
| | **demander qch à qn** | *to ask sb sth* |
| *from* | **arracher qch à qn** | *to snatch sth from sb* |
| | **acheter qch à qn** | *to buy sth from sb* |
| | **cacher qch à qn** | *to hide sth from sb* |
| | **emprunter qch à qn** | *to borrow sth from sb* |
| | **prendre qch à qn** | *to take sth from sb* |
| | **voler qch à qn** | *to steal sth from sb* |

| | | |
|---|---|---|
| descriptive | **la femme au chapeau vert** | *the woman with the green hat* |
| | **un garçon aux yeux bleus** | *a boy with blue eyes* |
| manner, means | **à l'anglaise** | *in the English manner* |
| | **fait à la main** | *handmade* |
| | **à bicyclette / cheval** | *by bicycle/on horseback* (BUT note other forms of transport used with **en** and **par**) |
| | **à pied** | *on foot* |
| | **chauffer au gaz** | *to heat with/by gas* |
| | **à pas lents** | *with slow steps* |
| | **cuisiner au beurre** | *to cook with butter* |
| time, date: *at, in* | **à minuit** | *at midnight* |
| | **à trois heures cinq** | *at five past three* |
| | **au 20ème siècle** | *in the 20th century* |
| | **à Noël/Pâques** | *at Christmas/Easter* |
| distance | **à 6 km d'ici** | *(at a distance of) 6 km from here* |
| | **à deux pas de chez moi** | *just a step from my place* |
| destined for | **une tasse à thé** | *a teacup* (compare **une tasse de thé**) |
| | **un service à café** | *a coffee service* |
| after certain adjectives | **son écriture est difficile à lire** | *his writing is difficult to read* (compare the usage with **de**, p. 206) |
| | **prêt à tout** | *ready for anything* |
| after certain verbs *Continued* | see p. 64 | |

## de

| | | |
|---|---|---|
| from | **venir de Londres** | *to come from London* |
| | **du matin au soir** | *from morning till night* |
| | **du 21 juin au 5 juillet** | *from 21st June till 5th July* |
| | **de 10 à 15** | *from 10 to 15* |
| belonging to, *of* | **un ami de la famille** | *a family friend* |
| | **les vents d'automne** | *the autumn winds* |
| contents, composition, material | **une boîte d'allumettes** | *a box of matches* |
| | **une tasse de thé** | *a cup of tea* (compare **une tasse à thé**) |
| | **une robe de soie** | *a silk dress* |
| manner | **d'une façon irrégulière** | *in an irregular way* |
| | **d'un coup de couteau** | *with the blow of a knife* |
| quality | **la société de consommation** | *the consumer society* |
| | **des objets de valeur** | *valuable items* |
| comparative + a number | **il y avait plus/moins de cent personnes** | *there were more/fewer than a hundred people* |
| after superlatives: *in* | **la plus/moins belle ville du monde** | *the most/least beautiful city in the world* |
| after certain adjectives | **surpris de voir** | *surprised to see* |
| | **il est difficile d'y accéder** | *access is difficult* (compare the usage with **à**, p. 205) |
| after certain verbs | see p. 64 | |

## en

| place: *to, in, on* | en ville<br>en pleine mer<br>en France | *in/to town*<br>*on the open sea*<br>*in/to France* (note that masculine countries use **à**) |
|---|---|---|
| dates, months: *in* | en 1923<br>en janvier | *in 1923*<br>*in January* |
| transport | en voiture<br>en avion | *by car*<br>*by plane* (but note usage of **à** and **par** in other expressions) |
| language | en français | *in French* |
| duration | je le ferai en trois jours | *I'll do it in three days* (i.e. *I'll take 3 days to do it*: compare **dans trois jours**) |
| material | un bracelet en or | *a bracelet made of gold* (note that the use of **en** stresses the material more than the use of **de**) |
| | consister en | *to consist of* |
| in the manner of, like a | parler en vrai connaisseur<br>déguisé en cowboy | *to speak like a real connoisseur*<br>*dressed up as a cowboy* |
| + present participle | il l'a vu en passant devant la porte | *he saw it as he came past the door* |

*Continued*

## avant

| | | |
|---|---|---|
| *before* | **il est arrivé avant toi** | *he arrived before you* |
| + infinitive (add **de**) | **je vais finir ça avant de manger** | *I'm going to finish this before eating* |
| preference | **la santé avant tout** | *health above all things* |

## chez

| | | |
|---|---|---|
| at the home of | **chez lui/moi** <br> **être chez soi** <br> **venez chez nous** | *at his/my house* <br> *to be at home* <br> *come round to our place* |
| *at/to* a shop | **chez le boucher** | *at/to the butcher's* |
| *in* a person, *among* a group of people or animals | **ce que je n'aime pas chez lui c'est son ...** <br> **chez les fourmis** | *what I don't like in him is his ...* <br> *among ants* |

## dans

| | | |
|---|---|---|
| position | **dans une boîte** | *in(to) a box* |
| circumstance | **dans son enfance** | *in his childhood* |
| future time | **dans trois jours** | *in three days' time* (compare **en trois jours**, p. 207) |

## depuis

| | | |
|---|---|---|
| *since*: time <br> place | **depuis mardi** <br> **il pleut depuis Paris** | *since Tuesday* <br> *it's been raining since Paris* |
| *for* | **il habite cette maison depuis 3 ans** | *he's been living in this house for 3 years* (NOTE TENSE) |

## dès

| | | |
|---|---|---|
| past time | **dès mon enfance** | *since my childhood* |
| future time | **je le ferai dès mon retour** | *I'll do it as soon as I get back* |

## entre

| | | |
|---|---|---|
| *between* | **entre 8 et 10** | *between 8 and 10* |
| *among* | **Jean et Pierre, entre autres** | *Jean and Pierre, among others* |
| reciprocal | **s'aider entre eux** | *to help each other (out)* |

## d'entre

| | | |
|---|---|---|
| *of, among* | **trois d'entre eux** | *three of them* |

## par

| | | |
|---|---|---|
| agent of passive: *by* | **renversé par une voiture** | *knocked down by a car* |
| | **tué par la foudre** | *killed by lightning* |
| weather conditions | **par un beau jour d'été** | *on a lovely summer's day* |
| *by (means of)* | **par un couloir/sentier** | *by a corridor/path* |
| | **par le train** | by train (but see also **à** and **en**) |
| | **par l'intermédiaire de M. Duval** | *through Mr. Duval* |
| distribution | **deux par deux** | *two by two* |
| | **par groupes de dix** | *in groups of ten* |
| | **deux fois par jour** | *twice a day* |

*Continued*

## pour

| | | |
|---|---|---|
| *for* | **c'est pour vous** | *it's for you* |
| | **c'est pour demain** | *it's for tomorrow* |
| | **une chambre pour 2 nuits** | *a room for 2 nights* |
| | **pour un enfant, il se débrouille bien** | *for a child he manages very well* |
| | **il part pour l'Espagne** | *he's leaving for Spain* |
| | **il l'a fait pour vous** | *he did it for you* |
| | **il lui a donné 50 francs pour ce livre** | *he gave him 50 francs for this book* |
| | **je ne suis pas pour cette idée** | *I'm not for that idea* |
| | **pour qui me prends-tu?** | *who do you take me for?* |
| | **il passe pour un idiot** | *he's taken for a fool* |
| + infinitive: *(in order) to* | **elle se pencha pour le ramasser** | *she bent down to pick it up* |
| | **c'est trop fragile pour servir de siège** | *it's too fragile to be used as a seat* |
| *to(wards)* | **être bon/gentil pour qn** | *to be kind to sb* |
| with prices, time | **pour 200 francs d'essence** | *200 francs' worth of petrol* |
| | **j'en ai encore pour une heure** | *I'll be another hour (at it) yet* |

## sans

| | | |
|---|---|---|
| *without* | **sans eau** | *without water* |
| | **sans ma femme** | *without my wife* |
| + infinitive | **sans compter les autres** | *without counting the others* |

## sauf

| | | |
|---|---|---|
| *except (for)* | **tous sauf lui** | *all except him* |
| | **sauf quand il pleut** | *except when its raining* |
| *barring* | **sauf imprévu** | *barring the unexpected* |
| | **sauf avis contraire** | *unless you hear to the contrary* |

## sur

| | | |
|---|---|---|
| *on* | **sur le siège** | *on the seat* |
| | **sur l'armoire** | *on top of the wardrobe* |
| | **sur le mur** | *on (top of) the wall* (if the meaning is *hanging on the wall* use **à**, p. 204) |
| | **sur votre gauche** | *on your left* |
| | **être sur le point de faire** | *to be on the point of doing* |
| *on (to)* | **mettez-le sur la table** | *put it on the table* |
| *proportion: out of, by* | **8 sur 10** | *8 out of 10* |
| | **un automobiliste sur 5** | *one motorist in 5* |
| | **la pièce fait 2 mètres sur 3** | *the room measures 2 metres by 3* |

## Conjunctions

There are conjunctions which introduce a main clause, such as **et** *and*, **mais** *but*, **si** *if*, **ou** *or* etc., and those which introduce subordinate clauses like **parce que** *because*, **pendant que** *while*, **après que** *after* etc. They are all used in much the same way as in English, but the following points are of note:

● Some conjunctions in French require a following subjunctive, see p. 58

● Some conjunctions are 'split' in French like *both ... and*, *either ... or* in English:

| | | |
|---|---|---|
| **et ... et** | *both ... and* | (→ 1) |
| **ni ... ni ... ne** | *neither ... nor* | (→ 2) |
| **ou (bien) .. ou (bien)** | *either ... or (else)* | (→ 3) |
| **soit ... soit** | *either ... or* | (→ 4) |

● **si** + **il(s)** → **s'il(s)** (→ 5)

● **que**
  – meaning *that* (→ 6)
  – replacing another conjunction (→ 7)
  – replacing **si**, see p. 62
  – in comparisons, meaning *as, than* (→ 8)
  – followed by the subjunctive, see p. 62

● **aussi** *so, therefore*: the subject and verb are inverted if the subject is a pronoun (→ 9)

**1** **Ces fleurs poussent et en été et en hiver**
These flowers grow in both summer and winter

**2** **Ni lui ni elle ne sont venus**
Neither he nor she came
**Ils n'ont ni argent ni nourriture**
They have neither money nor food

**3** **Elle doit être ou naïve ou stupide**
She must be either naïve or stupid
**Ou bien il m'évite ou bien il ne me reconnaît pas**
Either he's avoiding me or else he doesn't recognise me

**4** **Il faut choisir soit l'un soit l'autre**
You have to choose either one or the other

**5** **Je ne sais pas s'il vient/s'ils viennent**
I don't know if he's coming/if they're coming
**Dis-moi s'il y a des erreurs**
Tell me if there are any mistakes
**Votre passeport, s'il vous plaît**
Your passport, please

**6** **Il dit qu'il t'a vu**
He says (that) he saw you
**Est-ce qu'elle sait que vous êtes là?**
Does she know that you're here?

**7** **Quand tu seras plus grand et que tu auras une maison à toi, ...**
When you're older and you have a house of your own, ...
**Comme il pleuvait et que je n'avais pas de parapluie, ...**
As it was raining and I didn't have an umbrella, ...

**8** **Ils n'y vont pas aussi souvent que nous**
They don't go there as often as we do
**Il les aime plus que jamais**
He likes them more than ever
**L'argent est moins lourd que le plomb**
Silver is lighter than lead

**9** **Ceux-ci sont plus rares, aussi coûtent-ils cher**
These ones are rarer, so they're expensive

# Word Order

Word order in French is largely the same as in English, except for the following. Most of these have already been dealt with under the appropriate part of speech, but are summarised here along with other instances not covered elsewhere.

- Object pronouns nearly always come before the verb (→ **1**)
  For details, see pp. 166 to 170

- Certain adjectives come after the noun (→ **2**)
  For details, see p. 162

- Adverbs accompanying a verb in a simple tense usually follow the verb (→ **3**)
  For details, see p. 200

- After **aussi** *so*, *therefore*, **à peine** *hardly*, **peut-être** *perhaps*, the verb and subject are inverted (→ **4**)

- After the relative pronoun **dont** *whose* (→ **5**)
  For details, see p. 182

- In exclamations, **que** and **comme** do not affect the normal word order (→ **6**)

- Following direct speech:
  - the *verb + subject* order is inverted to become *subject + verb* (→ **7**)
  - with a pronoun subject, the verb and pronoun are linked by a hyphen (→ **8**)
  - when the verb ends in a vowel in the 3rd person singular, -t- is inserted between the pronoun and the verb (→ **9**)

For word order in negative sentences, see p. 216
For word order in interrogative sentences, see pp. 220 and 222

1 **Je les vois!**
　I can see them!

　**Il me l'a donné**
　He gave it to me

2 **une ville française**
　a French town

　**du vin rouge**
　some red wine

3 **Il pleut encore**
　It's still raining

　**Elle m'aide quelquefois**
　She sometimes helps me

4 **Il vit tout seul, aussi fait-il ce qu'il veut**
　He lives alone, so he does what he likes

　**A peine la pendule avait-elle sonné trois heures que ...**
　Hardly had the clock struck three when ...

　**Peut-être avez-vous raison**
　Perhaps you're right

5 Compare:　**un homme dont je connais la fille**
　　　　　　a man whose daughter I know

　and:　　**un homme dont la fille me connaît**
　　　　　a man whose daughter knows me

If the person (or object) 'owned' is the *object* of the verb, the order is:

**dont** + verb + noun (1st sentence)

If the person (or object) 'owned' is the *subject* of the verb, the order is:

**dont** + noun + verb (2nd sentence)

Note also:　**l'homme dont elle est la fille**
　　　　　　the man whose daughter she is

6 **Qu'il fait chaud!**
　How warm it is!

　**Que je suis content de vous voir!**
　How pleased I am to see you!

　**Comme c'est cher**
　How expensive it is!

　**Que tes voisins sont gentils!**
　How kind your neighbours are!

7 **'Je pense que oui'** a dit Luc
　'I think so,' said Luke

　**'Ça ne fait rien'** répondit Jean
　'It doesn't matter,' John replied

8 **'Quelle horreur!'** me suis-je exclamé
　'How awful!' I exclaimed

9 **'Pourquoi pas?'** a-t-elle demandé
　'Why not?' she asked

　**'Si c'est vrai,'** continua-t-il '...'
　'If it's true,' he went on '...'

# Negatives

| | |
|---|---|
| **ne ... pas** | *not* |
| **ne ... point** (literary) | *not* |
| **ne ... rien** | *nothing* |
| **ne ... personne** | *nobody* |
| **ne ... plus** | *no longer, no more* |
| **ne ... jamais** | *never* |
| **ne ... que** | *only* |
| **ne ... aucun(e)** | *no* |
| **ne ... nul(le)** | *no* |
| **ne ... nulle part** | *nowhere* |
| **ne ... ni** | *neither ... nor* |
| **ne ... ni ... ni** | *neither ... nor* |

● Word order

– In simple tenses and the imperative:
   **ne** precedes the verb (and any object pronouns) and the second
   element follows the verb (→ **1**)

– In compound tenses:
   i **ne ... pas, ne ... point, ne ... rien, ne ... plus, ne ...
     jamais, ne ... guère** follow the pattern:
     **ne** + auxiliary verb + **pas** + past participle (→ **2**)
   ii **ne ... personne, ne ... que, ne ... aucun(e), ne ... nul(le),
     ne ... nulle part, ne ... ni (... ni)** follow the pattern:
     **ne** + auxiliary verb + past participle + **personne** (→ **3**)

– With a verb in the infinitive:
   **ne ... pas, ne ... point** (etc. see i above) come together (→ **4**)

● For use of **rien**, **personne** and **aucun** as pronouns, see p. 178

*Continued*

1  **Je ne fume pas**
   I don't smoke
   **Ne changez rien**
   Don't change anything
   **Je ne vois personne**
   I can't see anybody
   **Nous ne nous verrons plus**
   We won't see each other any more
   **Il n'arrive jamais à l'heure**
   He never arrives on time
   **Il n'avait qu'une valise**
   He only had one suitcase
   **Je n'ai reçu aucune réponse**
   I have received no reply
   **Il ne boit ni ne fume**
   He neither drinks nor smokes
   **Ni mon fils ni ma fille ne les connaissaient**
   Neither my son nor my daughter knew them

2  **Elle n'a pas fait ses devoirs**
   She hasn't done her homework
   **Ne vous a-t-il rien dit?**
   Didn't he say anything to you?
   **Ils n'avaient jamais vu une si belle maison**
   They had never seen such a beautiful house
   **Tu n'as guère changé**
   You've hardly changed

3  **Je n'ai parlé à personne**
   I haven't spoken to anybody
   **Il n'avait mangé que la moitié du repas**
   He had only eaten half the meal
   **Elle ne les a trouvés nulle part**
   She couldn't find them anywhere
   **Il ne l'avait ni vu ni entendu**
   He had neither seen nor heard him

4  **Il essayait de ne pas rire**
   He was trying not to laugh

## .Negatives (ctd.)

● Combination of negatives.
These are the most common combinations of negative particles:

|  |  |
|---|---|
| **ne ... plus jamais** | (→ 1) |
| **ne ... plus personne** | (→ 2) |
| **ne ... plus rien** | (→ 3) |
| **ne ... plus ni ... ni ...** | (→ 4) |
| **ne ... jamais personne** | (→ 5) |
| **ne ... jamais rien** | (→ 6) |
| **ne ... jamais que** | (→ 7) |
| **ne ... jamais ni ... ni ...** | (→ 8) |
| **(ne ... pas) non plus** | (→ 9) |

**non** and **pas**
● **non** *no* is the usual negative response to a question (→ 10)
It is often translated as *not* (→ 11)
● **pas** is generally used when a distinction is being made, or for emphasis (→ 12)
It is often translated as *not* (→ 13)

1  **Je ne le ferai plus jamais**
   I'll never do it again

2  **Je ne connais plus personne à Rouen**
   I don't know anybody in Rouen any more

3  **Ces marchandises ne valaient plus rien**
   Those goods were no longer worth anything

4  **Ils n'ont plus ni chats ni chiens**
   They no longer have either cats or dogs

5  **On n'y voit jamais personne**
   You never see anybody there

6  **Ils ne font jamais rien d'intéressant**
   They never do anything interesting

7  **Je n'ai jamais parlé qu'à sa femme**
   I've only ever spoken to his wife

8  **Il ne m'a jamais ni écrit ni téléphoné**
   He has never either written to me or phoned me

9  **Ils n'ont pas d'enfants et nous non plus**
   They don't have any children and neither do we
   **Je ne les aime pas – Moi non plus**
   I don't like them – Neither do I; I don't either

10 **Vous voulez nous accompagner? – Non**
   Do you want to come with us? – No (I don't)

11 **Tu viens ou non?**
   Are you coming or not?
   **J'espère que non**
   I hope not

12 **Ma sœur aime le ski, moi pas**
   My sister likes skiing, I don't

13 **Qui a fait ça? – Pas moi!**
   Who did that? – Not me!
   **Est-il de retour? – Pas encore**
   Is he back? – Not yet
   **Tu as froid? – Pas du tout**
   Are you cold? – Not at all

## Question forms: direct

There are four ways of forming direct questions in French:

- by inverting the normal word order so that ·
  *pronoun subject + verb → verb + pronoun subject*.
  A hyphen links the verb and pronoun (→ **1**)

  – When the subject is a noun, a pronoun is inserted after the verb
    and linked to it by a hyphen (→ **2**)

  – When the verb ends in a vowel in the third person singular, **-t-** is
    inserted before the pronoun (→ **3**)
- by maintaining the word order *subject + verb*, but by using a rising
  intonation at the end of the sentence (→ **4**)

- by inserting **est-ce que** before the construction *subject + verb* (→ **5**)

- by using an interrogative word at the beginning of the sentence,
  together with inversion *or* the **est-ce que** form above (→ **6**)

1 **Aimez-vous la France?**
  Do you like France?
  **Est-ce possible?**
  Is it possible?
  **Part-on tout de suite?**
  Are we leaving right away?

  **Avez-vous fini?**
  Have you finished?
  **Est-elle restée?**
  Did she stay?

2 **Tes parents sont-ils en vacances?**
  Are your parents on holiday?
  **Jean-Benoît est-il parti?**
  Has Jean-Benoît left?

3 **A-t-elle de l'argent?**
  Has she any money?
  **La pièce dure-t-elle longtemps?**
  Does the play last long?
  **Mon père a-t-il téléphoné?**
  Has my father phoned?

4 **Il l'a fini**
  He's finished it
  **Robert va venir**
  Robert's coming

  **Il l'a fini?**
  Has he finished it?
  **Robert va venir?**
  Is Robert coming?

5 **Est-ce que tu la connais?**
  Do you know her?
  **Est-ce que tes parents sont revenus d'Italie?**
  Have your parents come back from Italy?

6 **Quel train** { **prends-tu?**
              { **est-ce que tu prends?**
  What train are you getting?
  **Lequel** { **est-ce que ta sœur préfère?**
          { **ta sœur préfère-t-elle?**
  Which one does your sister prefer?
  **Quand** { **êtes-vous arrivé?**
          { **est-ce que vous êtes arrivé?**
  When did you arrive?
  **Pourquoi** { **ne sont-ils pas venus?**
             { **est-ce qu'ils ne sont pas venus?**
  Why haven't they come?

## Question forms: indirect

An indirect question is one that is 'reported', e.g. he asked me *what the time was*, tell me *which way to go*. Word order in indirect questions is as follows:

● *interrogative word* + *subject* + *verb* (→ **1**)

● when the subject is a noun, and not a pronoun, the subject and verb are often inverted (→ **2**)

## n'est-ce pas

This is used wherever English would use *isn't it?*, *don't they?*, *weren't we?*, *is it?* etc. tagged on to the end of a sentence (→ **3**)

## oui and si

**Oui** is the word for *yes* in answer to a question put in the affirmative (→ **4**)
**Si** is the word for *yes* in answer to a question put in the negative or to contradict a negative statement (→ **5**)

1 **Je me demande s'il viendra**
  I wonder if he'll come
  **Je ne sais pas à quoi ça sert**
  I don't know what it's for
  **Dites-moi quel autobus va à la gare**
  Tell me which bus goes to the station
  **Il m'a demandé combien d'argent j'avais**
  He asked me how much money I had

2 **Elle ne sait pas à quelle heure commence le film**
  She doesn't know what time the film starts
  **Je me demande où sont mes clés**
  I wonder where my keys are
  **Elle nous a demandé comment allait notre père**
  She asked us how our father was
  **je ne sais pas ce que veulent dire ces mots**
  I don't know what these words mean

3 **Il fait chaud, n'est-ce pas?**
  It's warm, isn't it?
  **Vous n'oublierez pas, n'est-ce pas?**
  You won't forget, will you?

4 **Tu l'as fait? – Oui**
  Have you done it? – Yes (I have)

5 **Tu ne l'as pas fait? – Si**
  Haven't you done it? – Yes (I have)

## Numbers

| Cardinal (*one, two etc.*) | | Ordinal (*first, second etc.*) | |
|---|---|---|---|
| zéro | 0 | | |
| un (une) | 1 | premier (première) | 1er, 1ère |
| deux | 2 | deuxième, second(e) | 2ème |
| trois | 3 | troisième | 3ème |
| quatre | 4 | quatrième | 4ème |
| cinq | 5 | cinquième | 5ème |
| six | 6 | sixième | 6ème |
| sept | 7 | septième | 7ème |
| huit | 8 | huitième | 8ème |
| neuf | 9 | neuvième | 9ème |
| dix | 10 | dixième | 10ème |
| onze | 11 | onzième | 11ème |
| douze | 12 | douzième | 12ème |
| treize | 13 | treizième | 13ème |
| quatorze | 14 | quatorzième | 14ème |
| quinze | 15 | quinzième | 15ème |
| seize | 16 | seizième | 16ème |
| dix-sept | 17 | dix-septième | 17ème |
| dix-huit | 18 | dix-huitième | 18ème |
| dix-neuf | 19 | dix-neuvième | 19ème |
| vingt | 20 | vingtième | 20ème |
| vingt et un (une) | 21 | vingt et unième | 21ème |
| vingt-deux | 22 | vingt-deuxième | 22ème |
| vingt-trois | 23 | vingt-troisième | 23ème |
| trente | 30 | trentième | 30ème |
| quarante | 40 | quarantième | 40ème |
| cinquante | 50 | cinquantième | 50ème |
| soixante | 60 | soixantième | 60ème |
| soixante-dix | 70 | soixante-dixième | 70ème |
| soixante et onze | 71 | soixante-onzième | 71ème |
| soixante-douze | 72 | soixante-douzième | 72ème |
| quatre-vingts | 80 | quatre-vingtième | 80ème |
| quatre-vingt-un (une) | 81 | quatre-vingt-unième | 81ème |
| quatre-vingt-dix | 90 | quatre-vingt-dixième | 90ème |
| quatre-vingt-onze | 91 | quatre-vingt-onzième | 91ème |

## Numbers (ctd.)

| Cardinal | | Ordinal | |
|---|---|---|---|
| cent | 100 | centième | 100ème |
| cent un (une) | 101 | cent unième | 101ème |
| cent deux | 102 | cent deuxième | 102ème |
| cent dix | 110 | cent dixième | 110ème |
| cent quarante-deux | 142 | cent quarante-deuxième | 142ème |
| deux cents | 200 | deux centième | 200ème |
| duex cent un (une) | 201 | deux cent unième | 201ème |
| duex cent deux | 202 | deux cent-deuxième | 202ème |
| trois cents | 300 | trois centième | 300ème |
| quatre cents | 400 | quatre centième | 400ème |
| cinq cents | 500 | cinq centième | 500ème |
| six cents | 600 | six centième | 600ème |
| sept cents | 700 | sept centième | 700ème |
| huit cents | 800 | huit centième | 800ème |
| neuf cents | 900 | neuf centième | 900ème |
| mille | 1000 | millième | 1000ème |
| mille un (une) | 1001 | mille unième | 1001ème |
| mille deux | 1002 | mille deuxième | 1002ème |
| deux mille | 2000 | deux millième | 2000ème |
| cent mille | 100.000 | cent millième | 100.000ème |
| un million | 1.000.000 | millionième | 1.000.000ème |
| deux millions | 2.000.000 | deux millionième | 2.000.000ème |

| Fractions | | Others | |
|---|---|---|---|
| un demi, une demie | ½ | zéro virgule cinq | 0,5 |
| un tiers | ⅓ | un virgule trois | 1,3 |
| deux tiers | ⅔ | dix pour cent | 10% |
| un quart | ¼ | deux plus deux | 2 + 2 |
| trois quarts | ¾ | deux moins deux | 2 − 2 |
| un cinquième | ⅕ | deux fois deux | 2 × 2 |
| cinq et trois quarts | 5¾ | deux divisé par deux | 2 ÷ 2 |

Note the use of points with large numbers and commas with fractions, i.e. the opposite of English usage.

## Numbers: Other Uses

- -aine denoting approximate numbers:

| | |
|---|---|
| **une douzaine (de pommes)** | about a dozen (apples) |
| **une quinzaine (d'hommes)** | about fifteen (men) |
| **des centaines de personnes** | hundreds of people |
| BUT: **un millier (de voitures)** | about a thousand (cars) |

- measurements:

| | |
|---|---|
| **vingt mètres carrés** | 20 square metres |
| **vingt mètres cubes** | 20 cubic metres |
| **un pont long de quarante mètres** | a bridge 40 metres long |
| **avoir trois mètres de large / de haut** | to be 3 metres wide / high |

- miscellaneous:

| | |
|---|---|
| **Il habite au dix** | He lives at number 10 |
| **C'est au chapitre sept** | It's in chapter 7 |
| **(C'est) à la page 17** | (It's) on page 17 |
| **(Il habite) au septième étage** | (He lives) on the 7th floor |
| **Il est arrivé le septième** | He came in 7th |
| **échelle au vingt-cinq millième** | scale 1:25,000 |

## Telephone numbers

**Je voudrais Edimbourg trois cent trente, vingt-deux, dix**
I would like Edinburgh 330 22 10

**Je voudrais le soixante-cinq, treize, vingt-deux, zéro deux**
Could you get me 65 13 22 02

**Poste trois cent trente-cinq**
Extension number 335

**Poste vingt-deux, trente-trois**
Extension number 22 33

N.B. In French, telephone numbers are broken down into groups of two or three numbers (never four), and are not spoken separately as in English. They are also written in groups of two or three numbers.

## The calendar

**Dates**

**Quelle est la date d'aujourd'hui?** ⎫
**Quel jour sommes-nous?**           ⎬ What's the date today?

**C'est ...**         ⎫
**Nous sommes ...** ⎬ It's the ...
   **le premier février**        1st of February
   **le deux février**           2nd of February
   **le vingt-huit février**     28th of February


**Il vient le sept mars**     He's coming on the 7th of March

N.B. Use cardinal numbers except for the first of the month.

**Years**

**Je suis né en 1971**
I was born in 1971

**le douze février** ⎰ **dix-neuf cent soixante et onze**
          ⎱ **mil neuf cent soixante et onze**
(on) 12th February 1971

N.B. There are two ways of expressing the year (see last example).
Note the spelling of **mil** *one thousand* in dates.

**Other expressions**

| | |
|---|---|
| **dans les années cinquante** | during the fifties |
| **au vingtième siècle** | in the twentieth century |
| **en mai** | in May |
| **lundi (quinze)** | on Monday (the 15th) |
| **le lundi** | on Mondays |
| **dans dix jours** | in 10 days' time |
| **il y a dix jours** | 10 days ago |

## The Time

| **Quelle heure est-il?** | *What time is it?* |
|---|---|
| **Il est . . .** | *It's . . .* |

| | |
|---|---|
| 00.00 | **minuit** *midnight, twelve o'clock* |
| 00.10 | **minuit dix, zéro heure dix** |
| 00.15 | **minuit et quart, zéro heure quinze** |
| 00.30 | **minuit et demie, zéro heure trente** |
| 00.45 | **une heure moins (le) quart, zéro heure quarante-cinq** |

| | |
|---|---|
| 01.00 | **une heure du matin** *one a.m., one o'clock in the morning* |
| 01.10 | **une heure dix (du matin)** |
| 01.15 | **une heure et quart, une heure quinze** |
| 01.30 | **une heure et demie, une heure trente** |
| 01.45 | **deux heures moins (le) quart, une heure quarante-cinq** |
| 01.50 | **deux heures moins dix, une heure cinquante** |
| 01.59 | **deux heures moins une, une heure cinquante-neuf** |

| | |
|---|---|
| 12.00 | **midi, douze heures** *noon, twelve o'clock* |
| 12.30 | **midi et demie, douze heures trente** |

| | |
|---|---|
| 13.00 | **une heure de l'après-midi, treize heures** *one p.m., one o'clock in the afternoon* |
| 01.30 | **une heure et demie (de l'après-midi), treize heures trente** |

| | |
|---|---|
| 19.00 | **sept heures du soir, dix-neuf heures** *seven p.m., seven o'clock in the evening* |
| 19.30 | **sept heures et demie (du soir), dix-neuf heures trente** |

**A quelle heure venez-vous? – A sept heures**
What time are you coming? – At seven o'clock
**Les bureaux sont fermés de midi à quatorze heures**
The offices are closed from twelve until two
**à deux heures du matin/de l'après-midi**
at two o'clock in the morning/afternoon, at two a.m./p.m.
**à sept heures du soir**
at seven o'clock in the evening, at seven p.m.
**à cinq heures précises** *or* **pile**
at five o'clock sharp
**vers neuf heures**
about nine o'clock
**peu avant/après midi**
shortly before/after noon
**entre huit et neuf heures**
between eight and nine o'clock
**Il est plus de trois heures et demie**
It's after half past three
**Il faut y être à dix heures au plus tard/au plus tôt**
You have to be there by ten o'clock at the latest/earliest
**Ne venez pas plus tard que onze heures moins le quart**
Come no later than a quarter to eleven
**Il en a pour une demi-heure**
He'll be half an hour (at it)
**Elle est restée sans connaissance pendant un quart d'heure**
She was unconscious for a quarter of an hour
**Je les attends depuis une heure**
I've been waiting for them for an hour/since one o'clock
**Ils sont partis il y a quelques minutes**
They left a few minutes ago
**Je l'ai fait en vingt minutes**
I did it in twenty minutes
**Le train arrive dans une heure**
The train arrives in an hour('s time)
**Combien de temps dure ce film?**
How long does this film last?

Beware of translating word for word. While on occasion this is quite possible, quite often it is not. The need for caution is illustrated by the following:

- English phrasal verbs (i.e. verbs followed by a preposition) e.g. *to run away*, *to fall down* are often translated by one word in French (→ **1**)

- English verbal constructions often contain a preposition where none exists in French, or vice versa (→ **2**)

- Two or more prepositions in English may have a single rendering in French (→ **3**)

- A word which is singular in English may be plural in French, or vice versa (→ **4**)

- French has no equivalent of the possessive construction denoted by *--'s/--'s* (→ **5**)
  See also *at/in/to*, p. 234

## Specific problems

### -ing

This is translated in a variety of ways in French:

- *to be ...-ing* is translated by a simple verb (→ **6**)
  Exception: when a physical position is denoted, a past participle is used (→ **7**)

- in the construction *to see/hear sb ...-ing*, use an infinitive or **qui** + verb (→ **8**)

*-ing* can also be translated by:
  - an infinitive (→ **9**)
    (see p. 44)
  - a perfect infinitive (→ **10**)
    (see p. 46)
  - a present participle (→ **11**)
    (see p. 48)
  - a noun (→ **12**)

*Continued*

**1 s'enfuir**
to run away

**tomber**
to fall down

**céder**
to give in

**2 payer**
to pay for

**regarder**
to look at

**écouter**
to listen to

**obéir à**
to obey

**nuire à**
to harm

**manquer de**
to lack

**3 s'étonner de**
to be surprised at

**satisfait de**
satisfied with

**voler qch à**
to steal sth from

**apte à**
capable of; fit for

**4 les bagages**
the luggage

**ses cheveux**
his/her hair

**le bétail**
the cattle

**mon pantalon**
my trousers

**5 la voiture de mon frère**
my brother's car
(*literally: . . . of my brother*)

**la chambre des enfants**
the children's bedroom
(*literally: . . . of the children*)

**6 Il part demain**
He's leaving tomorrow

**Je lisais un roman**
I was reading a novel

**7 Elle est assise là-bas**
She's sitting over there

**Il était couché par terre**
He was lying on the ground

**8 Je les vois** $\left\{ \begin{array}{l} \textbf{venir} \\ \textbf{qui viennent} \end{array} \right\}$ I can see them coming

**Je l'ai entendue** $\left\{ \begin{array}{l} \textbf{chanter} \\ \textbf{qui chantait} \end{array} \right\}$ I heard her singing

**9 J'aime aller au cinéma**
I like going to the cinema

**Arrêtez de parler!**
Stop talking!

**Au lieu de répondre**
Instead of answering

**Avant de partir**
Before leaving

**10 Après avoir ouvert la boîte, il . . .**
After opening the box, he . . .

**11 Etant plus timide que moi, elle . . .**
Being shyer than me, she . . .

**12 Le ski me maintient en forme**
Skiing keeps me fit

## to be

● Generally translated by **être** (→ **1**)
  When physical location is implied, **se trouver** may be used (→ **2**)

● In set expressions, describing physical and emotional conditions,
  **avoir** is used:

| | |
|---|---|
| **avoir chaud/froid** | *to be warm/cold* |
| **avoir faim/soif** | *to be hungry/thirsty* |
| **avoir peur/honte** | *to be afraid/ashamed* |
| **avoir tort/raison** | *to be wrong/right* |

● Describing the weather, e.g. *what's the weather like?*, *it's
  windy/sunny*, use **faire** (→ **3**)

● For ages, e.g. *he is 6*, use **avoir** (→ **4**)

● For state of health, e.g. *he's unwell, how are you?*, use **aller** (→ **5**)

## it is, it's

● Usually **il/elle est**, when referring to a noun (→ **6**)

● For expressions of time, also use **il est** (→ **7**)

● To describe the weather, e.g. *it's windy*, see above

● In the construction: *it is difficult/easy to do sth*, use **il est** (→ **8**)

● In all other constructions, use **c'est** (→ **9**)

## there is/there are

● Both are translated by **il y a** (→ **10**)

## can, be able

● Physical ability is expressed by **pouvoir** (→ **11**)

● If the meaning is *to know how to*, use **savoir** (→ **12**)

● *Can* + a 'verb of hearing or seeing etc.' in English is not translated in
  French (→ **13**)

1 **Il est tard**
It's late

**C'est peu probable**
It's not very likely

2 **Où se trouve la gare?**
Where's the station?

3 **Quel temps fait-il?**
What's the weather like?

**Il fait beau/mauvais/du vent**
It's lovely/miserable/windy

4 **Quel âge avez-vous?**
How old are you?

**J'ai quinze ans**
I'm fifteen

5 **Comment allez-vous?**
How are you?

**Je vais très bien**
I'm very well

6 **Où est mon parapluie? – Il est là, dans le coin**
Where's my umbrella? – It's there, in the corner
**Descends la valise si elle n'est pas trop lourde**
Bring down the case if it isn't too heavy

7 **Quelle heure est-il? – Il est sept heures et demie**
What's the time? – It's half past seven

8 **Il est difficile de répondre à cette question**
It's difficult to reply to this question

9 **C'est moi qui ne l'aime pas**
It's me who doesn't like him
**C'est Charles/ma mère qui l'a dit**
It's Charles/my mother who said so
**C'est ici que je les ai achetés**
It's here that I bought them
**C'est parce que la poste est fermée que ...**
It's because the post office is closed that ...

10 **Il y a quelqu'un à la porte**
There's somebody at the door
**Il y a cinq livres sur la table**
There are five books on the table

11 **Pouvez-vous atteindre cette étagère?**
Can you reach up to that shelf?

12 **Elle ne sait pas nager**
She can't swim

13 **Je ne vois rien**
I can't see anything

**Il les entendait**
He could hear them

**to** (see also below)

● Generally translated by **à** (→ **1**)
(See p. 204)

● In time expressions, e.g. *10 to 6*, use **moins** (→ **2**)

● When the meaning is *in order to*, use **pour** (→ **3**)

● Following a verb, as in *to try to do, to like to do*, see pp. 44 and 64

● *easy/difficult/impossible* etc. *to do*:
The preposition used depends on whether a specific noun is referred to (→ **4**) or not (→ **5**)

## at/in/to

● With feminine countries, use **en** (→ **6**)
With masculine countries, use **au** (**aux** with plural countries) (→ **7**)

● With towns, use **à** (→ **8**)

● *at/to the butcher's/grocer's* etc.: use **à** + noun designating the shop, or **chez** + noun designating the shopkeeper (→ **9**)

● *at/to the dentist's/doctor's* etc.: use **chez** (→ **10**)

● *at/to . . .'s/. . .s' house*: use **chez** (→ **11**)

**1 Donne le livre à Patrick**
Give the book to Patrick

**2 dix heures moins cinq**          **à sept heures moins le quart**
five to ten                          at a quarter to seven

**3 Je l'ai fait pour vous aider**
I did it to help you
**Il se pencha pour nouer son lacet**
He bent down to tie his shoelace

**4 Ce livre est difficile à lire**
This book is difficult to read

**5 Il est difficile de comprendre leurs raisons**
It's difficult to understand their reasons

**6 Il est allé en France / en Suisse**
He has gone to France/to Switzerland
**un village en Norvège / en Belgique**
a village in Norway/in Belgium

**7 Etes-vous allé au Canada / au Danemark / aux Etats-Unis?**
Have you been to Canada/to Denmark/to the United States?
**une ville au Japon / au Brésil**
a town in Japan/in Brazil

**8 Il est allé à Vienne / à Bruxelles**
He has gone to Vienna/to Brussels
**Il habite à Londres / à Genève**
He lives in London/in Geneva
**Ils logent dans un hôtel à St. Pierre**
They're staying in a hotel at St. Pierre

**9 Je l'ai acheté** { **à l'épicerie** / **chez l'épicier** }  I bought it at the grocer's
**Elle est allée** { **à la boulangerie** / **chez le boulanger** }  She's gone to the baker's

**10 J'ai un rendez-vous chez le dentiste**
I've an appointment at the dentist's
**Il est allé chez le médecin**
He has gone to the doctor's

**11 chez Christian**          **chez les Pagot**
at/to Christian's house      at/to the Pagots' house

# General Points

- Activity of the lips
  The lips play a very important part in French. When a vowel is described as having 'rounded' lips, the lips are slightly drawn together and pursed, as when an English speaker expresses exaggerated surprise with the vowel 'ooh!'. Equally, if the lips are said to be 'spread', the corners are pulled firmly back towards the cheeks, tendng to reveal the front teeth.

  In English, lip position is not important, and vowel sounds tend to merge because of this. In French, the activity of the lips means that every vowel sound is clearly distinct from every other.

- No diphthongs
  A diphthong is a glide between two vowel sounds in the same syllable. In English, there are few 'pure' vowel sounds, but largely diphthongs instead. Although speakers of English may *think* they produce one vowel sound in the word 'day', in fact they use a diphthong, which in this instance is a glide between the vowels [e] and [ɪ]: [deɪ]. In French the tension maintained in the lips, tongue and the mouth in general prevents diphthongs occurring, as the vowel sound is kept constant throughout. Hence the French word corresponding to the above example, 'dé', is pronounced with no final [ɪ] sound, but is phonetically represented thus: [de].

- Consonants
  In English, consonants are often pronounced with a degree of laxness that can result in their practically disappearing altogether although not strictly 'silent'. In a relaxed pronunciation of a word such as 'hat', the 't' is often scarcely heard, or is replaced by a 'glottal stop' (a sort of jerk in the throat). This never occurs in French, where consonants are always given their full value.

## Pronunciation of Consonants

Some consonants are pronounced almost exactly as in English: [b, p, f, v, g, k, m, w].
Most others are similar to English, but slight differences should be noted.

| EXAMPLES | HINTS ON PRONUNCIATION |
|---|---|
| [d] **d**inde | |
| [t] **t**ente | The tip of the tongue touches the upper front teeth and not the roof of the mouth as in English |
| [n] **n**onne | |
| [l] **L**i**ll**e | |
| | |
| [s] tou**s ç**a | The tip of the tongue is down behind the bottom front teeth, lower than in English |
| [z] **z**éro ro**s**e | |
| | |
| [ʃ] **ch**ose ta**ch**e | Like the *sh* of English *shout* |
| [ʒ] **j**e **g**ilet bei**g**e | Like the *s* of English *measure* |
| [j] **y**eux pai**ll**e | Like the *y* of English *yes* |

Three consonants are not heard in English:

| | |
|---|---|
| [ʀ] **r**are veni**r** | *R* is often silent in English, e.g. fa*r*m. In French the [ʀ] is never silent, unless it follows an **e** at the end of a word e.g. cherch**er**. To pronounce it, try to make a short sound like gargling. Similar, too, to the Scottish pronunciation of lo*ch* |
| [ŋ] vi**gn**e a**gn**eau | Similar to the *ni* of Spa*ni*ard |
| [ɥ] **h**uile l**u**eur | Like a very rapid [y] (see p. 239) followed immediately by the next vowel of the word |

## Pronunciation of Vowels

|             | EXAMPLES | HINTS ON PRONUNCIATION |
|---|---|---|

[a] **pa**tte pl**a**t **a**mour — Similar to the vowel in English *pat*

[ɑ] b**a**s p**â**te — Longer than the sound above, it resembles the English exclamation of surprise *ah!* Similar, too, to the English vowel in *car* without the final *r* sound

[ɛ] l**ai**t jou**e**t m**e**rci — Similar to the English vowel in *pet*. Beware of using the English diphthong [eɪ] as in *pay*

[e] **é**t**é** jou**e**r — A pure vowel, again quite different from the diphthong in English *pay*

[ə] l**e** pr**e**mier — Similar to the English sound in butt**er** when the *r* is not pronounced

[i] **i**c**i vie** l**y**cée — The lips are well spread towards the cheeks while uttering this sound. Shorter than the English vowel in *see*

[ɔ] m**o**rt h**o**mme — The lips are well rounded while producing a sound similar to the *o* of English *cot*

[o] m**o**t d**ô**me **eau** — A pure vowel with strongly rounded lips; quite different from the diphthong in English *bone*, *low*

| | |
|---|---|
| [u] gen**ou** r**ou**e | A pure vowel with strongly rounded lips. Similar to the English *ooh!* of surprise |
| [y] r**ue** vêt**u** | Often the most difficult for English speakers to produce: round your lips and try to pronounce [i] (see above). There is no [j] sound (see p. 237) as there is in English *pure* |
| [œ] s**œu**r b**eu**rre | Similar to the vowel in English *fir* or *murmur*, but without the *r* sound and with the lips more strongly rounded |
| [ø] p**eu** d**eu**x | To pronounce this, try to say [e] (see above) with the lips strongly rounded |

**Nasal Vowels**

These are spelt with a vowel followed by a 'nasal' consonant – **n** or **m**. The production of nasal vowels really requires the help of a teacher or a recording of the sound. However, to help you, the vowel is pronounced by allowing the air from the lungs to come partly down the nose and partly through the mouth, and the **n** or **m** is not pronounced at all.

| | |
|---|---|
| [ɑ̃] l**en**t s**an**g d**an**s | |
| [ɛ̃] mat**in** pl**ein** | In each case, the vowel shown in the phonetic symbol is pronounced as described above, but air is allowed to come through the nose as well as the mouth |
| [ɔ̃] n**on** p**on**t | |
| [œ̃] br**un un** parf**um** | |

## From Spelling to Sounds

Although it may not seem so at first sight, there are some fairly precise 'rules' which can help you to know how to pronounce French words from their spelling.

### Vowels

| SPELLING | PRONOUNCED | EXAMPLES |
|---|---|---|
| **a, à** | [a] | cha tte, ta ble |
| **a, â** | [ɑ] | pâte, pas |
| **e, é** | [e] | été, marcher |
| **e, é, ê** | [ɛ] | fenêtre, fermer, chère |
| **e** | [ɔ]ˑ | double, fenêtre |
| **i, î, y** | [i] | lit. abîmer, lycée |
| **o, ô** | [o] | pot, trop, dôme |
| **o** | [ɔ] | sotte, orange |
| **u, û** | [y] | battu, fût, pur |

### Vowel Groups

There are several groups of vowels in French spelling which are regularly pronounced in the same way:

| | | |
|---|---|---|
| **ai** | [ɛ] or [e] | maison, marchai, faire |
| **ail** | [aj] | portail |
| **ain, aim, (c)in, im** | [ɛ̃] | pain, faim, frein, impair |
| **au** | [o] | auberge, landau |
| **an, am, en, em** | [ɑ̃] | plan, ample, entrer, temps |
| **eau** | [o] | bateau, eau |
| **eu** | [œ] or [ø] | feu, peur |
| **euil(le), ueil** | [œj] | feuille, recueil |
| **oi, oy** | [wa] | voire, voyage |
| **on, om** | [ɔ̃] | ton, compter |
| **ou** | [u] | hibou, outil |
| **œu** | [œ] | sœur, cœur |
| **ue** | [y] | rue |
| **un, um** | [œ̃] | brun, parfum |

Added to these are the many groups of letters occurring at the end of
words, where their pronunciation is predictable, bearing in mind the
tendency (see p. 242) of final consonants to remain silent:

| *TYPICAL WORDS* | *PRONUNCIATION OF FINAL SYLLABLE* |
|---|---|
| **pas, mât, chat** | [ɑ] or [a] |
| **marcher, marchez**<br>**marchais, marchait,**<br>**baie, valet, mes, fumée** | [e] or [ɛ] |
| **nid** | [i] |
| **chaud, vaut, faux,**<br>**sot, tôt, Pernod, dos, croc** | [o] |
| **bout, bijoux, sous, boue** | [u] |
| **fut, fût, crus, crûs** | [y] |
| **queue, heureux, bleus** | [ø] |
| **en, vend, vent,**<br>**an, sang, grand, dans** | [ã] |
| **fin, feint, frein, vain** | [ɛ̃] |
| **on, pont, fond, avons** | [ɔ̃] |
| **brun, parfum** | [œ̃] |

*Continued*

## From Spelling to Sounds (ctd.)

## Consonants

● Final consonants are usually silent (→1)

● **n** or **m** at the end of a syllable or word are silent, but they have the effect of 'nasalizing' the preceding vowel(s) (see p. 239 on Nasal Vowels)

● The letter **h** is either 'silent' ('mute') or 'aspirate' when it begins a word. When silent, the word behaves as though it started with a vowel and takes a liaison with the preceding word where appropriate.
When the **h** is aspirate, no liaison is made (→2)
There is no way of predicting which words start with which sort of **h** – this simply has to be learnt with each word

● The following consonants in spelling have predictable pronunciations: b, d, f, k, l, p, r, t, v, w, x, y, z. Others vary:

| SPELLING | PRONOUNCED | ENGLISH EXAMPLES | |
|---|---|---|---|
| **c + a, o, u**<br>**+ l, r** | [k] | can, cot, cut<br>class, cram | (→3) |
| **c + e, i, y** | [s] | ceiling, ice | (→4) |
| **ç + a, o, u** | [s] | ceiling, ice | (→5) |
| **ch** | [ʃ] | shop, lash | (→6) |
| **g + a, o, u**<br>**+ l, r** | [g] | gate, got, gun<br>glass, gramme | (→7) |
| **g + e, i, y** | [ʒ] | leisure | (→8) |
| **gn** | [ŋ] | companion, onion | (→9) |
| **j** | [ʒ] | measure | (→10) |
| **q, qu** | [k] | quay, kit | (→11) |
| **s** between vowels:<br>elsewhere | [z]<br>[s] | rose<br>sit | (→12) |
| **th** | [t] | Thomas | (→13) |
| **t** in **-tion** | [s] | sit | (→14) |

**1 éclat**
[ekla]

**nez**
[ne]

**chaud**
[ʃo]

**aider**
[ɛde]

**2 silent h:**

**aspirate h:**

**des hôtels**
[de zotɛl]

**des haricots**
[de aʀiko]

**3 café**
[kafe]

**côte**
[kot]

**culture**
[kyltyʀ]

**classe**
[klas]

**croûte**
[kʀut]

**4 ceci**
[səsi]

**cil**
[sil]

**cycliste**
[siklist]

**5 ça**
[sɑ]

**garçon**
[gaʀsɔ̃]

**déçu**
[desy]

**6 chat**
[ʃa]

**riche**
[ʀiʃ]

**7 gare**
[gaʀ]

**gourde**
[guʀd]

**aigu**
[ɛgy]

**glaise**
[glɛz]

**gramme**
[gʀam]

**8 gemme**
[ʒɛm]

**gilet**
[ʒilɛ]

**gymnaste**
[ʒimnast]

**9 vigne**
[viŋ]

**oignon**
[ɔŋɔ̃]

**10 joli**
[ʒɔli]

**Jules**
[ʒyl]

**11 quiche**
[kiʃ]

**quitter**
[kite]

**12 sable**
[sablə]

**maison**
[mɛzɔ̃]

**13 théâtre**
[teɑtʀ]

**Thomas**
[tɔma]

**14 nation**
[nasjɔ̃]

**action**
[aksjɔ̃]

## Feminine Forms and Pronunciation

● For adjectives and nouns ending in a vowel in the masculine, the addition of an **e** to form the feminine does not alter the pronunciation (→**1**)

● If the masculine ends with a silent consonant, generally **-d**, **-s**, **-r** or **-t**, the consonant is sounded in the feminine (→**2**)
This also applies when the final consonant is doubled before the addition of the feminine **e** (→**3**)

● If the masculine ends in a nasal vowel and a silent **n**, e.g. **-an**, **-on**, **-in**, the vowel is no longer nasalized and the **-n** is pronounced in the feminine (→**4**)
This also applies when the final **-n** is doubled before the addition of the feminine **e** (→**5**)

● Where the masculine and feminine forms have totally different endings (see pp. 136 and 150), the pronunciation of course varies accordingly (→**6**)

## Plural Forms and Pronunciation

● The addition of **s** or **x** to form regular plurals generally does not affect pronunciation (→**7**)

● Where liaison has to be made, the final **-s** or **-x** of the plural form is pronounced (→**8**)

● Where the masculine singular and plural forms have totally different endings (see pp. 138 and 148), the pronunciation of course varies accordingly (→**9**)

● Note the change in pronunciation in the following nouns:

| SINGULAR | | PLURAL | | |
|----------|--------|--------|-------|-------------|
| **bœuf** | [bœf] | **bœufs** | [bø] | *ox/oxen* |
| **œuf** | [œf] | **œufs** | [ø] | *egg/eggs* |
| **os** | [ɔs] | **os** | [o] | *bone/bones* |

*ADJECTIVES*

**1 joli** → **jolie**
[ʒɔli]     [ʒɔli]
**déçu** → **déçue**
[desy]     [desy]
**2 chaud** → **chaude**
[ʃo]     [ʃod]
**français** → **française**
[frãsɛ]     [frãsɛz]
**inquiet** → **inquiète**
[ɛ̃kjɛ]     [ɛ̃kjɛt]
**3 violet** → **violette**
[vjɔlɛ]     [vjɔlɛt]
**gras** → **grasse**
[grɑ]     [grɑs]
**4 plein** → **pleine**
[plɛ̃]     [plɛn]
**fin** → **fine**
[fɛ̃]     [fin]
**brun** → **brune**
[brœ̃]     [bryn]
**5 canadien** → **canadienne**
[kanadjɛ̃]     [kanadjɛn]
**breton** → **bretonne**
[brətɔ̃]     [brətɔn]
**6 vif** → **vive**
[vif]     [viv]
**traître** → **traîtresse**
[trɛtrə]     [trɛtrɛs]
**7 beau** → **beaux**
[bo]     [bo]
**8 des anciens élèves**
[de zãsjɛ̃ zelɛv]
**de beaux arbres**
[də bo zarbr(ə)]
**9 amical** → **amicaux**
[amikal]     [amiko]

*NOUNS*

**un ami** → **une amie**
[ami]     [ami]
**un employé** → **une employée**
[ãplwaje]     [ãplwaje]
**un étudiant** → **une étudiante**
[etydjã]     [etydjãt]
**un Anglais** → **une Anglaise**
[ãglɛ]     [ãglɛz]
**un étranger** → **une étrangère**
[etrãʒe]     [etrãʒɛr]
**le cadet** → **la cadette**
[kadɛ]     [kadɛt]
→
**le souverain** → **la souveraine**
[suvrɛ̃]     [suvrɛn]
**Le Persan** → **la Persane**
[pɛrsã]     [pɛrsan]
**le voisin** → **la voisine**
[vwazɛ̃]     [vwazin]
**le paysan** → **la paysanne**
[peizã]     [peizan]
**le baron** → **la baronne**
[barɔ̃]     [barɔn]
**le veuf** → **la veuve**
[vœf]     [vœv]
**le maître** → **la maîtresse**
[mɛtrə]     [mɛtrɛs]
**la maison** → **les maisons**
[mɛzɔ̃]     [mɛzɔ̃]

**un journal** → **des journaux**
[ʒurnal]     [ʒurno]

## The Alphabet

| | | | | | | |
|---|---|---|---|---|---|
| **A, a** | [ɑ] | **J, j** | [ʒi] | **S, s** | [ɛs] |
| **B, b** | [be] | **K, k** | [ka] | **T, t** | [te] |
| **C, c** | [se] | **L, l** | [ɛl] | **U, u** | [y] |
| **D, d** | [de] | **M, m** | [ɛm] | **V, v** | [ve] |
| **E, e** | [ə] | **N, n** | [ɛn] | **W, w** | [dubləve] |
| **F, f** | [ɛf] | **O, o** | [o] | **X, x** | [iks] |
| **G, g** | [ʒe] | **P, p** | [pe] | **Y, y** | [igRɛk] |
| **H, h** | [aʃ] | **Q, q** | [ky] | **Z, z** | [zɛd] |
| **I, i** | [i] | **R, r** | [ɛr] | | |

Capital letters are used as in English *except* for the following:

● adjectives of nationality
  e.g. **une ville espagnole**    **un auteur français**
  a Spanish town    a French author

● languages
  e.g. **Parlez-vous anglais?**    **Il parle français et allemand**
  Do you speak English?    He speaks French and German

● days of the week:

| | |
|---|---|
| **lundi** | Monday |
| **mardi** | Tuesday |
| **mercredi** | Wednesday |
| **jeudi** | Thursday |
| **vendredi** | Friday |
| **samedi** | Saturday |
| **dimanche** | Sunday |

● months of the year:

| | | | |
|---|---|---|---|
| **janvier** | January | **juillet** | July |
| **février** | February | **août** | August |
| **mars** | March | **septembre** | September |
| **avril** | April | **octobre** | October |
| **mai** | May | **novembre** | November |
| **juin** | June | **décembre** | December |

The following index lists comprehensively both grammatical terms and key words in French and English contained in this book.